CHURCH FOLK

A NOVEL

BY

J. MOFFETT WALKER

ISBN: 0-75961-051-7

This book is printed on acid free paper.

Quoted scriptures with references are from the Holy Bible, Ziegler
and McCurdy, 1872.

1stBooks – rev. 09/13/01

DEDICATION

I dedicate this novel to my husband, Tommy Walker, Sr., my best friend, companion and consultant.

Further, I dedicate this book to my sons: Tommy, Jr., Edward and Roland; my granddaughters: Shree, Shreece; my late goddaughter and niece Evette Monai Lyles, Pharm. D.

To my parents the late Fred Douglas Moffett, Sr. and Matlean Allen Moffett, I am grateful for your visions and my religious upbringing.

I give God Almighty thanks for giving me a good life, all the above mentioned, including the ambition to be forever creative.

Acknowledgements

Sincere and grateful acknowledgements to: Dorthy J. Burnett, resource person; William Drozda, social studies teacher, James Holloway, art teacher; Bobbie Jones, Naomi Lyles, and Tommy L. Walker, Sr., consultants; Jamal Rasheed, author; Malita Moore, Deborah Parker, and Tommy L Walker, Jr., young adult consultants.

Church Folk is a creation of the author's imagination. All characters are fictional.

PROLOGUE

Historically, the Black church as an institution evolved itself to help shape and direct lives spiritually, morally and socially. Church...well, it has been the backbone for strong Blacks from slavery village days to the new African-American community. To put it a different way, Black churches have provided soul medicine for its members helping them learn to cope in the ever-changing American society.

Unfortunately, too many local, state, and national leaders in the Christian Living Baptist churches have failed to uphold the principles the founders established for the church. Some religious leaders across state lines, too, bog themselves down with their own immoral concerns and self-greed, rejecting sound religious commitment. What irony of purpose and function!

Church Folk raised issues about the corruption within the Christian Living Baptist churches and the complacency that usually goes along with it. Yet, it seems no one wants to be accountable for the morally declining churches and society as a whole. Likewise, leaders everywhere model for the children, teenagers and young adults whatever the fashion. Moreover, the younger generations have a need to see adults consistently model wholesome, clean, everyday living.

On the other hand, have Christian Living Baptist parishioners stopped the emotional roller coasters long enough to think about the inner happenings of their religious world? Do members understand the moralistic impact of selecting irresponsible leaders? Do members understand the obligation to hold leaders accountable? When leaders fail to uphold religious principles and decent morals, do parishioners confront them or rubber-stamp the leaders' wrongs? Do members realize the effect Christian leaders, good or bad, have on real people...children, grandchildren, congregations, communities and society? Simply put from another angle, are Christian Living Baptist Church members focused on spirituality? In other words, why do members go to church? Do members go to church for entertainment as if attending a play in a theater? Do members go for physical exercise as if attending a dance in a juke hall? Do any members show up to hear singing as if attending a concert in an auditorium with stained glass windows? More importantly, do members attend church for appropriate spiritual guidance? Do members want to know what thus saith the Lord to serve mankind?

Additionally, in which way should Christian Living Baptist ministers, the leaders of congregations, help society with moral issues? Should parishioners begin by selecting leaders who have exemplary morals themselves? After all, they will be the ones who choose to include or exclude a particular community program. Moreover, can a minister with embedded unresolved immoral issues practice moral authority with his flock? Besides, if religious leaders of congregations are not morally fit, then who…?

Beyond morality, another issue must be solved. Is training for Christian Living Baptist ministers a reasonable concern? Admittedly, some trained ministers will be ineffective. But a leader with a mixture of sound morals, a willing heart and a reasonable level of training can more likely meet the needs of the membership and serve the community well. For example, what level of help, if any, can a non-trained minister offer to his flock on issues such as drug, alcohol, spousal and or sexual abuse? Imagine the level of counseling that minister will offer to single parents and their families, gays, divorcees, pregnant teens, high school drop-outs and those unemployed. I raised this training issue because inappropriate counseling can be detrimental to those seeking help. What would an untrained Christian Living Baptist male minister tell a female in his flock who aspired to become a minister in the church? Would he quote I Corinthians 14:34 out of historical religious context? In the meantime, issues such as these walk right through the doors of all Christian Living Baptist churches each Sunday morning and on Tuesdays, too, if the doors are opened. Help for those in need must go far beyond recognizing the issues and addressing them in a creatively prepared or a highly emotional extemporaneous sermon.

"STUDY TO SHEW THYSELF APPROVED UNTO GOD A WORKMAN WHO DOES NOT NEED TO BE ASHAMED, HANDLING ACCURATELY THE WORD OF TRUTH." (II Timothy 2:15)

Think about the number of times the above scripture is quoted. Yet, the leader who spoke those words may have had difficulty reading the popular passage, let alone understanding it on a level other than literal. Above all, the Christian Living Baptists must now seek to solve issues like these discussed in this book, if the organization plans to remain in tact and be effective in the new millenium.

Surely, this book addresses morality versus immorality, politics versus religion, but this roadmap reveals what happens to a functional church when self-greed and ignorance prevail.

Chapter 1

March 03, 1986

"All members please remain for a short meeting," stated Harry Smith, chairman of the Pulpit Committee.

Worship service went extremely well that day.

A near capacity crowd had gathered to witness with mere presence, to praise and adore Him, the Almighty God. With songs and prayer, the congregation joined together harmoniously asking for His strength and guidance for another week's journey.

Deacon Smith not only chaired the Pulpit Committee (PC), he chaired the Deacon Board (DB) and the Finance Committee (FC).

A visiting minister preached a sermon, which sent an electric-like spiritual charge all through hungry souls.

The weather, fairly warm in Grand Rapids, Michigan, had a temperature range somewhere in the high sixties. Great weather I'd say for a March day in a city almost inside the roaring Lake Michigan.

It had to be an emergency meeting to be held on a Sunday, the same day, I thought.

My name is Juanna Walton, a member of the congregation.

Church of Heaven (C.O.H), the church where the spirit of Christian minds is like to Him above, enjoyed a sweet, sweet spirit. In fact, peace, love, unity and unspeakable joy filled the air.

Besides that, we thought we had the valued quality called respect. Visitors who came our way said the air permeated those Christian ideals.

The choir could be heard each Sunday morning echoing words from that old Baptist hymnal, *There's a sweet, sweet spirit in this place.*

Most members knew our church had the right *stuff* in the walls of our house. We felt proud!

Charter members experienced a previous church in deep disarray with demon-like divisions.

They even went through low-down name-calling and heated fussing with ghetto-like *cussing*. I guess it could be said members fought at Grand Bulah as if with the help of vodka or gin. Several leaders toted guns to save themselves and their church friends.

Members at C.O.H. left all that behind.

Grand Bulah's former pastor of fifty years retired and relocated to Vicksburg, Mississippi.

Fairly large, with a membership of 500, Grand Bulah once competed to be the Christian Living Baptist Church in Grand Rapids. But unresolved issues about the pastor's contract caused the division. Members, who believed Grand Bulah's leadership failed to uphold sound Christian principles, left.

C.O.H. celebrated an anniversary a few Sundays earlier. As part of the establishment, the new church pledged forever to display Christian-like behavior. Charter members and those who joined the new church years later kept the unwritten code of ethics. The church family lived and breathed this sacred vow!

"Will the meeting now come to order?" Chairman Smith announced.

We assembled quickly, quietly, but not questionably.

Minutes of a church meeting held in December showed that the body overwhelmingly elected a pastor. Members most eagerly awaited the arrival of the Rev. Sam Clark, Fort Wayne, Indiana, who caught the attention of the parishioners and received the required 55% votes on his first try.

Deacon Smith informed us a few Sundays before that the pastor-elect would begin his duties in March.

I did not see this as unrealistic. Rev. Clark was teaching a Bible class at a local college in Fort Wayne.

I felt that we needed a morally sound pastor. Furthermore, I thought we needed an informed, progressive, seminary-trained minister.

At a prior church meeting, one member said, *"We need a family man."*

The membership responded with a big, loud *"AMEN!"*

Our congregation had ordinary people both married and single: grandparents, parents, retirees, counselors, nurses, factory employees, teachers, social workers, and mail carriers, and yes, welfare recipients too.

Nothing extraordinary about the people or their careers existed. Erin Myles, my twenty-four year old niece and goddaughter, had just become our first registered pharmacist. But for the record, no lawyer or medical doctor worshipped in our congregation. To my knowledge, no member in our church studied law, but my son, Ronald, a first year medical student, pledged to become our first doctor.

At any rate, Rev. Leroy Jamison, Rev. Clark's opponent, lost his third attempt to become pastor.

Rev. Clark, married with four teenage children, had begun to make plans to relocate.

Not everyone thought Rev. Clark deserved to pastor C.O.H.

"He is too educated," according to Deacon Wilson, a college educated janitor.

"We can't afford him," commented Trustee Carr, a retired postman.

"He can't preach," said Deacon Barnes, a retired hospital worker.

O, what quietness...! Well, if a piece of cotton had fallen on the carpeted section of the church floor, sharp eyes would surely have seen it, and inquiring ears might have imagined a quite loud bumpty, bumpty, bumpty, bump!

Deacon Smith continued, "Will those Joint Board members who agreed with the Pulpit Committee's actions, please stand with me?"

Joint Board (JB) members consisted of all twelve deacons and twenty trustees.

By now thoughts of all kinds floated throughout the sanctuary.

3

Seemingly, few JB members knew about this action. My eyebrows raised and parted too, when I noticed most JB members remained in their seats!

However, eight deacons, two trustees and one *wanna be* deacon answered the call: Deacons Michael Harris, Larry Wilson, Eugene Allen, T. J. Johnson, Walter Cousins, Billy Packson, Ezekiel Barnes, James Hatly; Trustees Lincoln Carr, Sam Johnson and Pearl Sanders.

Eleven rose, walked to the front of the church, and stood with Deacon Smith.

Now Smith, a neat, one-eyed tall man, dressed in a single-breasted navy blue suit, breathed a sigh of relief and smiled.

"What is this?" I thought.

"Is this tyranny?" a Christian soul sitting directly behind me shouted.

Frustrations like these bounced in many minds.

Smith, who looked to be about forty, out of nowhere, began the deacon chairperson's position, just before our former pastor left.

Rev. Richardson, our former pastor, resigned to assume pastoral duties at a larger church, St. Jude.

Although the deacon board election was due a year later, the officials reorganized. Why this happened, I do not know. I certainly did not understand why all the board members allowed it to take place.

A college graduate and a computer analyst, Smith failed to go through the normal chairperson's rank. He never experienced vice-chairman of the board. He paid no seniority dues. In fact, Smith, a clean-headed man, could be called *a babe in Christ,* but members trusted him.

Anyone who had been with us for a few years or longer remembered when Smith got religion, joined, was baptized, ate and drank his first communion, sang in the Senior Choir, took over financial responsibilities and later became a deacon.

Actually, with Smith's PC duties, most members thought he lived up to his responsibilities. Smith completed a year of what looked to have been reasonable leadership appearing open and fair.

Deacon Smith continued in an unsure, quivering voice, "I speak for all the members of the PC. We would like to inform the church that we completed our task. We prayed individually and collectively. We followed our church selection process and *Robert's Rules of Order*. The PC changed the other candidate on the last ballot to pastor of C.O.H. His name is Rev. Leroy Jamison."

A trillion hands flew up!

Then he said, "This meeting is adjourned."

"What the **hell** did Smith say?" someone asked.

"Deacon Smith! Deacon Smith! Deacon Smith!" came from everywhere.

Stunned, angry, disappointed and mad members jumped up to confront Deacon Smith.

"I'll be **damned**!" I heard those curse words with my own ears ringing, right out in our sacred, church sanctuary. Cold-blooded Smith and those betrayers, who stood with the leaders, rushed away abruptly without uttering a single sound to anyone.

"Those good-for-nothing so-and-so's forced that three time loser on us," one member said.

"Since when can deacons in a Christian Living Baptist Church make a candidate a pastor, just like that?" A deep thinker reflected.

"Oh no!" I cried. "What a disgrace, what injustice!" I continued. Although dispirited at first, within minutes I began to forget about the corrupted officials and my discomfort with their deceptions. I managed to meditate on these elegant words:

"...INASMUCH AS YE HAVE DONE IT UNTO ONE OF THE LEAST OF THESE MY BRETHREN, YOU HAVE DONE IT UNTO ME." (Matthew 25:40)

Chapter 2

March 10, 1986

Members sat on a plush, white sofa or in blue chairs, as their eyes met other decorative trimmings. The Simpson's home made a lovely setting for the thirty-five unhappy members who attended the first planning meeting. Now Mrs. Sarah Simpson, an immaculate housekeeper and physical education teacher, had mastered the skills of being a career person, mother, and modern wife while maintaining her self-identity.

Despite numerous telephone calls to Deacon Smith's work place, the church office and his home, Smith refused to return calls. None of the deacons on the PC, who stood with him, would discuss the matter. They all behaved as if no one could touch what they had done.

"They vowed not to talk to any of you," said Diane Cousins, wife of Deacon Cousins, as she left the March 3rd meeting.

A medium size congregation, with about three hundred members on roll, we had one hundred fifty active members. So, most knew where each other stood on the pastor selection issue.

I spoke to Deacon Harris, myself, as he stormed out the edifice that March Sunday.

"Deacon Harris," I said, "how can you do this to your Christian brothers and sisters and have a clear conscious?" He just gave me a sly look, blinked his eyes, made his way around me, and kept on walking.

Six other church officials knew the PC had overstepped their boundaries and misused their leadership positions. Trustees Randall Stove, Barney Lee, Andy Robinson, Maya McNair, Howard Morner, and Thomas Walton; deacons Bernard Simpson, Ezell Fields, Edwin Savannah and Jack Savannah, decided to work with those who believed they had been misused and abused.

"Father God, lead us through our troubles; we need you, Lord, to hear our prayer. Father God, just guide us! But, Father God, direct us to a peaceful solution to our deep concern. Father God, we know you can. Amen," began Deacon Simpson.

Selina Savannah asked, "Can they get away doing that?"

Mrs. Savannah's emotions ran even higher than others did. Her husband, Charles Savannah, had wholeheartedly accepted and supported the PC's actions.

Selina's heart hurt!

Trustee Stove expressed his views, "Can we get a lawyer?"

"Yes," came from all directions in loud tones.

Trustee Walton and Deacon Simpson discussed a few days earlier the possibility of organizing a group to hire a legal person to help sort out feelings from facts and decide what action, if any, a group could take. Although unable to attend the first meeting, Walton did commit himself to stand firm.

Other families besides Selina and her husband divided on this issue. Deacon Edwin Savannah, Selina's father-in-law and mother-in-law joined in to correct the wrong. Deacon Jack Savannah, Charles' uncle and his wife Laura supported the cause. One of Charles' uncles who had not been to church too much during the last ten years, showed up at church to give his approval to the PC. Twelve of my family members joined the protest. However, my sister Lorene supported the PC.

Four hours later the meeting ended. Deacons Simpson and Fields had already chosen a lawyer. They announced to the group, "Attorney Josset Brown is the one!"

A church sister, Susie, 83, now deceased, wrote a $500 check. "I can get more where that came from," said the old, upset senior in a trembling voice. Well, the first meeting…a $3,500 blessing!

We loved C. O. H. so much that everyone hoped Deacon Smith would wake up and say, "I'm sorry; let's meet. Please forgive!"

"PRESERVE ME O GOD: FOR IN THEE DO I PUT MY TRUST." (Psalm 16:1)

Chapter 3

June 18, 1962

On this blessed day, June 18, 1962, C.O.H. moved into the church building located in midtown, at the crossroad of Hope and Harsh, 911 Hope Street.

What a hallelujah good day!

Built in 1920, Catholics had once owned the edifice and recreation center.

Like most inner cities, a few whites had begun fleeing for the suburbs.

Alpine, Edgerton, and Kent became the places to live for those who wanted to exit.

Naming the church, Church of Heaven, became an easy matter. The founders intended it to be forever a house of the Lord, an extension of the past, but a safe place for participation and community fellowship.

The group named Rev. Terrance Hill, Jr. pastor and founder during the third planning session. Although the confusion and split at Grand Bulah developed during the senior Rev. Terrance Hill's stay, this group knew his son, a young, gifted man, had exemplary leadership skills.

Rev. Hill, Jr. had marched with Dr. Melvin L. Cain, Jr. in Atlanta, Georgia. Once Rev. Hill went to jail while participating in a demonstration march for civil rights.

What used to be a Catholic cathedral now became a home for Christian Living Baptists! The majestic building had a huge belfry with a top-centered, rustic, wrought iron bell. What a masterpiece!

Each window showed a play of white, yellow and purple, stained glass, rich looking. The red brick church gave the now C.O.H. a real classic look.

Inside the structure, one's eyes met two main Roman columns. Later on those same eyes focused on magnificent religious murals in bold gold, blue and red. One mural depicted the resurrection of Christ, and another showed a religious council at work. What beauty!

On any given Sunday one marveled at church participants, especially children, looking at the paintings.

Rev. Hill brought with him, his wife Glenda, an attractive woman with light brown skin and long, curly hair, blue-gray eyes and a model figure. Our first family had two very young girls, ages three and four. When Glenda met Rev. Hill at a civil rights activity, she had already begun a professional acting career. But love has a way of making a lady change her career, put a career on hold or not even think about a career for a while. Needless to say, Glenda chose to become a preacher's wife.

That day the Senior Choir came into the sanctuary right after the deacons completed the devotion: prayer, scripture and the *Doctor Watts*. Now the *Doctor Watts* song began a long time ago in Black churches when one or two men in a congregation could read. The reader would recite a few words, give a meter or tune to match the words and the whole congregation sang proudly.

"Must Jesus bear the cross alone, and all the world go free." The group would sing. Then the leader would say, "No, there is a cross for everyone, and there's a cross for me." The congregation then completed the verse.

At the end of the devotion, the full Senior Choir, nearly one hundred voices, came in marching to a beat, singing loudly, but in four parts, *Step to Jesus*. The singers paraded from the back, down the center aisles to the front, two deep, stepping, slightly rocking, in any Sunday's best national Black folk's church uniform, with the ladies wearing black skirts and white blouses and with the men wearing black pants, white shirts with black string ties.

A large crowd filled the pews; some even sat in the balcony. Those who sat in the balcony watched the finest details. They saw the leg and foot actions of the organist and pianist and the hand-held fans across the audience going from right to left, right to left, to and

9

fro, to and fro, where parishioners fanned trying to get relief from the heat in the non-air conditioned sanctuary.

Regardless of what Rev. Hill preached, regardless of how long he preached, nothing could have gone wrong that day, absolutely nothing! That day the church called *Thank-You Jesus Day!*

Chapter 4

July 03, 1974

Can a church make a real difference in a community? Rev. Hill and this church did in just three years with grass root outreach programs.

All C.O.H had was a group of about forty-five committed members who turned the church into approximately 400 members in thirty-six months.

Rev. Hill's leadership skills helped to place C.O.H. on the United States map. While in college, he involved himself with the Peace Committee and the Freedom Travelers.

His past involvement gave him insight of people and their problems, not just church problems or Black people's problems. The pastor rallied for human and civil rights. He taught fairness, respect, and responsibility. You know about the good old values needed in life to be successful. He believed in feeding his flock with everyday spiritual needs, not robbing them by preaching outdated concepts and ideas his flock could not understand or could not use in their daily lives.

Sometimes Rev. Hill's philosophy, however, landed trouble for him and his congregation.

One day Rev. Hill met with some young men of the community. You might call them *thugs*. But anyway the group was impressed with Rev. Hill's message and their perception of him.

"We need warriors to work for Jesus Christ," Pastor Hill replied.

They gave their individual attention.

"Christ objected to humans trying to keep other humans down," Rev. Hill said. "Jesus dislikes sins. For example, stealing is a sin," he went on to say.

The next day Rev. Hill noticed somebody had placed the church's three stolen typewriters back on the stands where they belonged.

On several occasions Rev. Hill's open door policy {unlocked doors at the church and center} made it easy for criminals to do their thing, walk away with church property.

What a unique inner city Black church!

For the first time in a Grand Rapids church, adults and children could enroll in karate, free of charge. C.O.H. began a class teaching the art of passing from teenage years to young adulthood. Pastor Hill understood the need to help teens learn about stages they pass through before becoming adults. He tried to help. Later on C.O.H. established a newsletter, *Information,* which gave us political attention.

Rev. Hill knew his young adult membership had senior parents. He knew the young would grow old. So, C.O.H. established a geriatric class.

C.O.H. quickly operated a multi-faceted ministry rather than the usual everyday Sunday school, 11:00 a.m. worship and Wednesday night prayer meeting church.

Even then, Pastor Hill saw the need for *a dope church,* organized services for drug addicts. He wanted the users to realize how their present habits helped to create their own plights.

Rev. Hill, a rather heavyset, dark skinned man, knew politics as well as religion. He stood six feet tall and about the same in necessary people skills.

The congregation named their adjacent building the Berry-Calton Center, upon the recommendations of Rev. Hill. He had worked with Jerry Berry of Georgia and had learned much from Matthew Calton, then president of Elder College in Louisiana where Rev. Hill had been formally trained.

A proud time came when the National Church Council selected us as one of the top fifty churches in the United States and one of the top ten Black churches in America for our innovative programs.

Only as a result of Pastor Hill's leadership and the willingness of the congregation, these accomplishments occurred.

The council included us in, *Churches In America*, a television show aired on local and national airwaves, starring the wife of a deacon, Mary Johnson; the wife of a trustee, Goldia Morner, both Sunday school teachers and a choir member, Roberta Jones, singing a modern version of *Amazing Grace*!

No other church in Grand Rapids, old or young had achieved this recognition. We rejoiced!

Helpers' Business Center that Rev. Hill introduced to his followers gave training in nursing, basic education, consumer education, job search, and personal development. It helped to train the unemployed.

Robert Wills, a widower for many years, served as chairman of the Deacon Board. Deacon Wills, a stately looking sophisticated man, could be trusted to lead the spiritual group. He was a man of principles.

Although not the chairman while at Grand Bulah, he served on the board. Everybody at our church respected him. In fact, he had gained citywide respect and recognition for community service.

With such an outstanding beginning, how could anything go wrong? Everyone appeared safe, happy and relaxed with his or her church experiences.

Deacon Wills reported to the board, " Our pastor wants to talk to us."

"About what?" Deacon Simpson responded.

"I'm not sure, but he will meet with us after Sunday school today," replied Deacon Wills.

"Yes, let him explain the situation to us," uttered Deacon E. Savannah.

After Sunday school that day, the board and the pastor did meet.

"Pastor," stated Deacon Wills, "is there a concern that you want to discuss with us?"

"Thank you, Deacon Wills, I wish it were not true."

The board went limp. No one knew what to say. "I am offering my resignation effective today," stated the pastor.

Silence took over. Most of the twelve men broke down and sobbed like young infants.

Worship went as usual! Everyone thought so, except for the deacons.

During the devotion the deacons sang and prayed and prayed and sang! Deacon Wills and several other deacons broke down again and again, but no one suspected anything.

Roberta directed our Senior Choir. The group sang at its best. This time the choir wore their long, royal blue robes.

Rev. Hill asked, "Will all members remain after service for a short church meeting?" He dismissed the visitors as all members reassembled.

"Today, July 3, 1964, I have submitted my resignation to the deacons to be effective immediately," Pastor Hill explained.

I'm sure he felt he did the Christian thing for the good of the church. But, by then, everyone had begun sobbing!

"Oh no!" Roberta cried.

"I love you and wish you God's continued success!" said Pastor Hill.

Then he left the pulpit.

Some prayed; some kept silent; some stared; some expressed disbelief while others stood just plain old dumbfounded!

The disappointed group accepted the pastor's resignation!

Chapter 5

September 5, 1974

Wills often quoted, **"TRUST IN THE LORD WITH ALL THINE HEART, AND LEAN NOT TO THINE OWN UNDERSTANDING. IN ALL THY WAYS ACKNOWLEDGE HIM, AND HE SHALL DIRECT THY PATHS."** (Proverbs 3: 5-6)

I always believed Deacon Wills considered this his favorite scripture.

No one could push Deacon Wills over or around; still, he had a tremendous load to carry. He now needed all the experience he had gained from working at Grand Bulah and all he had gained from working with former Pastor Hill.

We depended on his leadership to hold the church together.

Mature, trustworthy and responsible best describe Deacon Wills, but how could the members forget what had happened at Grand Bulah?

Rev. Hill, his wife and their two grade school daughters lived in a fairly new apartment complex. The church had not acquired a parsonage.

C.O.H. members never knew what really happened. The officers believed that some type serious threats were being made on the pastor and his family. At any rate, no one, however, questioned that the pastor needed to protect his family.

Deacon Wills and the PC began looking for someone with skills like Hill's to lead the church.

Chapter 6

March 26, 1965

I need Thee every hour, most gracious Lord.
No tender voice like Thine can peace afford.
I need Thee, O, I need Thee;
Every hour I need Thee! O bless me now, my Savior, I come to
Thee!

Rev. Ward began his sermons with the mighty words from this familiar hymn. As soon as he arrived, the membership learned quickly that our new pastor could deliver a spirited message.

Capable church leaders and a well-informed minister organized our church, but also the members worked together for the good of the organization.

Deacon Wills followed the church's constitution for pastoral selection with pride. He had too much respect for himself, his fellow members and God to do otherwise.

On March 26, 1965, the church elected Rev. Eric Ward of Georgia. Although not unanimous, the majority, the constitutional requirement, voted for Rev. Ward.

Everyone expected adjustments. In fact, who would blame a new leader for making some changes?

Rev. Ward, who had just graduated from Elder College in Louisiana, the same college where Rev. Hill studied, also understood the works and function of a church and its organizations. The deacons provided the spiritual nourishment. The trustees cared for all church property; the missionaries ministered to the needy; the choir provided the music ministry; the ushers showed hospitality to all.

We began a Sunday night weekly radio broadcast service that proved good for a congregation that had had a satisfying taste of community involvement. The air service gave us something to talk about, something to do and a chance to reach the sick and shut-in with community feedback.

The other ministries were no different from the other churches' programs.

Rev. Hill's era had ended and all his programs too.

Not everybody understood the new leader. He did appear rather uptight. He tried not to be too friendly. I supposed he did that because he had an old man's job.

He greeted members quite formally. He appeared less personable than the former pastor. Some members had a real difficult time accepting that. A few members called our pastor Rev. Dictator.

Lincoln Carr and his wife Francis left and joined a church near Muskegon. Mrs. Carr had worked in various capacities in the church: usher board, special project director and youth director. No one could say she did not have talent. Besides, this church sister volunteered most of her services.

The church set about forty miles east of C.O.H. No member felt the Carrs liked their new church home that well. Close friends and relatives felt that they would surely return to C.O.H.

Mrs. Carr's two cousins, Darlene and Maya and four nieces stayed at C.O.H. Francis's aunt, a stately, wise woman who reared her, remained at Grand Bulah. Mrs. Carr's uncle-in-law, husband of her aunt, had been accidentally killed in a local factory during the fifties.

Sister Fannie Sanders endured four years of unhappiness. Rarely did she utter a good word about Rev. Ward.

Short, somewhat overweight and fair-skinned, this church lady proved to be quite literate in the academics, but church members talked mostly about her personal interactions with others.

"The church did not cause her frustrations," commented Jerry, an older, wiser member. "Her family did. She worries about her children." At that time, two young adult sons had gotten into trouble with the law. For the most part, the young men were good young men. They grew up in the church. We, her church family, empathized.

The deacons loved the pastor, followed him everywhere he requested and gave him anything he wanted. That started some controversy. For the first time the deacons gave the pastor a Master Card. With this card came few, if any, restrictions.

Tracy Myles once visited her home in Jackson, Tennessee. Guess whom she saw and what she saw?

Pastor Ward was holding hands with a beautiful, young lady in Jackson. He saw Tracy, too, and played it off. Surely, soon afterward Pastor Ward announced he would wed Julia Walls. C.O.H. loved that! We needed a first lady.

Then he said, "Yes, Mrs. Myles, I saw you in Jackson."

Rev. Ward's pastorage did meet heated controversy. He recommended dismissal of the entire Robinson family.

Pete and Lillie Mae Robinson played a major role in organizing C.O.H. They gave liberal monetary contributions and their services too. Mr. and Mrs. Robinson owned a wig shop where business flourished.

The deacons agreed to dismiss the sons but rejected Rev. Ward's request to dismiss their parents.

Rev. Ward claimed those dismissed had been harassing him.

Timothy played the church organ. Could he make music!

Bobbie said, "He makes that organ talk to me." He loved the instrument!

His brother Teddy had a unique baritone voice. He sang in the Senior Choir.

Excommunication has never been an accepted practice in the Christian Living Baptist Church, despite its inclusion in some church by-laws. Our founders included excommunication. Those who supported the officials quoted the constitution.

Many choir members hated to lose two talented young men. What could they do? About thirty choir members organized a community gospel choir to fill the void. They called the new group Inspirational Non-Denomination. Our church choir members decided if the Non-Denoms had an engagement the same date and time as their church choir, they would choose to go with the Non-Denoms.

So, most choir members protested! The board didn't like it; Rev. Ward didn't like it but....

"Tim, your volunteer services aren't needed here," said Rev. Ward.

Timothy and his brother Teddy stopped coming.

Members later learned one of the Robinson brothers supposedly clashed with Rev Ward while at Elder College.

The young men's parents hurt without help from the church leadership or membership. The Robinsons had worked side by side with the church leadership from the beginning to this point. Actually, the church began in the Robinsons' home.

Timothy, according to Pastor Ward, called him a punk. Rev. Ward's emotions boiled!

Mr. and Mrs. Robinson stayed with the church of their love, but they directed their tithes to the bank.

"I can't reward anyone for wrong doings," stated Mrs. Robinson. "School business should remain at school."

"I don't know what happened, but the once student now pastors a congregation; he needs to grow up," replied the men's father.

After several problems, relationships slowly began to decline from bad to worse.

Another member, Juanita Allen, who grew up under Rev. Hill, informed Rev. Ward she would wed soon. Jubilant, at first, but when she requested Rev. Hill's return to assist with the wedding ceremony, Rev. Ward flatly said, "No, no way!" Somehow he felt Rev. Hill's assistance would be disrespectful to him.

It wasn't long before Rev. Ward accepted a church in Tennessee. Therefore, he submitted his resignation. By then even the deacons knew the time had come for our pastor to move on. And he did!

Again, C.O.H. found itself without a pastor. The Robinsons released thousands of dollars of withheld tithes! Lincoln and Francis returned! But the Robinson men, C.O.H. lost forever!

Chapter 7

September 30, 1969

"You elected the Rev. Leroy Jamison," declared Deacon Wills.

Leadership, this time, shifted to a person with a memorable personality and an almost million dollar smile. Rev. Jamison quoted scriptures and delivered memorized messages. Besides, he had a clear quartet-like, strong bass voice.

His fair skin and straight hair made one believe he was not an African-American at first sight. But, when he opened his mouth all doubt....

The Deacon Board controlled the pastoral candidates. The membership made a selection based entirely on the persons the PC brought to the church. Members, limited to the information the committee wanted the church to know, voted on the candidates.

Rev. Jamison, who began his tenure in the fall, had attended Edwards Junior Baptist College during the 60's. How long...well, that was never clear.

In many ways the new pastor differed from Rev. Ward and Rev. Hill. Hill proved a well-prepared, progressive pastor; Ward was a good speaker and impersonal leader, but Jamison established his ministry like an actor, singer, and an interesting entertainer.

Rev. Jamison amazed his congregation, like a character does in a play, but without cue cards or a singer does on stage without music. He spoke every word just as he had planned it. Now one may or may not have agreed with what he prepared in his sermons, but most would agree that he delivered pretty darn well what he had memorized. Often he ended his sermons with one of his favorite songs such as *The Lord Will Make A Way Somehow*. He touched many souls with that song.

"He repeats his sermons too much," voiced Bobbie. Sometimes the Sundays came too often to memorize a sermon. His staunch supporters didn't seem to care what he did! They loved him, whether he repeated a sermon or not.

Not so for Bobbie!

"I heard him the first time," Bobbie said. She came up with a plan, which she discussed with her pastor. "Rev. Jamison, anytime you repeat a sermon , I will choose to leave, go home or visit another church."

From the choir stand I watched Bobbie each Sunday as Rev. Jamison announced his text, to see if she removed herself from the place.

Right away the church began to prosper.

Former members reunited with the church and brought relatives and friends with them who joined.

Rev. Jamison hailed from the good southern state of Mississippi, bringing a fairly new bride and two pre-teen boys from a previous marriage. The boys, we soon learned, did not live with our pastor and our first lady except during the summer. They resided with their mom back in Edwards, Mississippi.

Rev. Jamison recommended a prison ministry. We responded with a weekly prayer, scripture and praise service at the Correctional Center in Kalamazoo. I joined in, along with my three sisters, to provide four-part Black gospel music for the male inmates every fifth Saturday afternoon. The minister of music, Rev. Harry Richards, accompanied us on piano. Other church members volunteered their services too.

Participants followed the regular rules of **search and strip** as anyone does visiting a prison.

The prison ministry touched me because I knew someone incarcerated in another state. I felt, somehow, my participation would help me learn through first-hand experiences about the lives of inmates in a hard-core American prison.

After receiving clearance, we led the prisoners in religious worship. Usually this consisted of songs such as *What a Friend or Pass Me Not,* reading a scripture and giving a spiritual lecture. We presented our special music just before the message and immediately following it.

While on my first trip, a young male church participant named James, explained this to the prisoners:

"If you pimp or prostitute, be the best little pimp or prostitute you can be."

What a message! Did he represent my church? I had heard about things like this going on behind prison walls. But, here I came to portray our society, a Christian Living Baptist Church, a lady, a wife and a parent. I could not condone this!

When I returned home, I reported to the pastor what the member had said. Nothing became of it to my knowledge.

The church continued to prosper. By then we grossed $250,000 annually with less than 300 members.

Dianna said to Mrs. Simpson, "Our first lady is pregnant."

And before long, Rev. Jamison announced the good news from the pulpit.

"Church, God is so good; my wife Bobbi and I have learned we are expecting a baby." The church was right with him.

"Amen!"

"It's a girl! " our pastor announced.

"Amen," again, the audience shouted.

They called her Little Mary even before she made her entrance.

Grand Rapids local Preachers' Association voted Rev. Jamison *Mr. Character*. His recognition pleased him. It delighted us too.

One Sunday the congregation boarded a bus to visit a church in Milwaukee, Wisconsin. The pastor of that church was our pastor's friend. Rev. Jamison stated as he took the pulpit:

"I'm not wearing these shades because it's cute. My doctor informed me on yesterday that my eyes are extra sensitive to light." Only silence spoke!

We had a wonderful fellowship with that congregation, Love Feast Church, Rev. Otis Carson, Pastor. After the 11:00 a.m. services, the host church served a tasty dinner downstairs in their cafeteria: string beans, fried chicken, cornbread, peach cobbler, coffee, pop, and of course white and chocolate milk. I can taste it now! The food satisfied our stomachs!

Chapter 8

August 09, 1974

During Rev. Jamison's tenure we had a popular choir. The members included professional and self-taught musicians, singers, and directresses.

I guess I fell some place in the self-taught...singers, musicians.

Roberta, a natural born and university-trained singer, presented free concerts for the community. Roberta's voice could fill the edifice and sooth a heavy heart any day of the week.

She sang for the late Ted O'Nell, the late, then Honorable Vice-President Wallace Mondell during their separate visits to the city.

Roscoe Grand, a baritone, proved to be no exception. His voice jerked thousands of our tears on a given Sunday.

Unlike Roberta, Roscoe could not read a note or even request a particular key signature. However, the Rev. Richards, who graduated from State University in Mississippi with a degree in music, had all of that under control. He knew what songs to ask Roscoe to sing and when he needed to sing. What musicians!

During Richards' leadership, I led several songs. He even left me in charge of the choir a few Sundays.

Now the Senior Choir did not function without upheavals. Take for example, one male member dated several ladies in the choir. That caused conflicts among the involved ladies.

Choir members who thought alike on a particular issue grouped together for support. This especially occurred before and during our major concerts. Several sopranos clashed for leadership roles in songs.

Three choir members sang their way through college, Selina, Lorene and Roberta. Now, do you see the talent?

One day in a youth meeting, a youngster asked, "Why does Rev. Jamison say you don't need an education?"

"I don't think he meant that," commented Mrs. Myles.

24

"Oh, yes, he did!" the child reemphasized.

"My teacher told me at school one day that if I didn't learn to read, I could become a preacher, misread the Bible and mislead our people," said another child.

"Why did she say that? " the child further inquired.

"Can you think of a reason why she said that?" Mrs. Myles replied.

"I think she hates preachers trying to tell her what to do," the first child uttered.

The second youth spoke again, "Maybe, too many Black preachers read poorly and refuse to get help."

"Do you plan to stay in school?" Mrs. Myles inquired.

"Yes, ma'am," the youth responded.

Our congregation had its own invisible divisions. Most members came from the South: Alabama, Arkansas, Georgia, Louisiana, Mississippi, Tennessee and Missouri. However, being a good Christian has nothing to do with one's original home state, career or social standing.

Approximately two-thirds of the members worked hard labor jobs but faired well economically! Those members contributed their ten percent to the church.

However, before those members left the South, they sharecropped and did not have the opportunity to complete the eighth grade, or high school.

"There just was no time for school," I often heard.

I knew that statement spoke the truth. But, God smiled on his people, allowing them to relocate to Grand Rapids and prosper.

It takes many types of occupations and workers to have a functional community. Nevertheless, the laborers expressed a feeling about the one third of the church that one day would damage relationships.

"You educated people think you is better than us."

We often heard statements like this. Sometimes speakers implied it.

"I ain't stupid!"

This attitude came from the pulpit to the back pew.

And, the educated people took the emotional abuse.

Sermons, speeches and comments kept coming as if to make the educated feel inferior and inadequate in the Christian aspect of life.

We understood.

Other times someone would say, "I wish I could have had training."

The pendulum began swinging from harmony and unity to the educated verses the uneducated.

How sad!

But I did not feel that I should apologize for my parents' insight and my determination to succeed in school. Instead, that made me realize how much the youth of our church needed Christian guidance and direction from those who had it to give. Maybe we failed to give the adult members, who express these views, the moral support they needed.

"Educated fools," rang out.

"I didn't rub my head up against no college wall."

I understood!

"We may not have a B.S. degree, but we have a **Jesus degree**."

A Jesus degree? In that case, some members have both.

I didn't understand the comparison of an uneducated Christian to a formally educated one.

A Christian is a Christian. Judge not by trade but by one's actions, I thought.

I got stuck with, "**STUDY TO SHEW THYSELF APPROVED**."

The only difference I could see…well, the trained person, college or self-taught, possibly could read the most complicated book in the world, the Bible, with some understanding.

Besides, this education issue brought back memories about my foreparents. My late maternal grandfather, a Christian Living Baptist deacon, could not read. In fact, my maternal grandmother, his wife, didn't know her own name when flashed before her face.

But they broke the illiteracy chain! They made sure their daughter, Mattie, my mother, now ninety, a retired teacher, learned to read before she began school. It took hard work raising cotton, corn, potatoes, peas, and peanuts sharecropping in Tennessee to send Mother to a private high school. Besides, one-half of their profit went to the landowner.

Well, other members had similar situations.

Hopefully, the Christian adults did not confuse the young members, teenagers and children, about the value of an education.

Did I hear *training requires hard work*? Did I hear *education cannot be forced on anyone, but it helps one to live a decent, quality life*? *Did I hear*, would *you put forth the effort, time*? Did I hear *a good education helps one become a well-informed Christian*?

I began to wonder…does a portion of the Christian Living Baptist Church leadership encourage their members to accept the leaders' understanding about church, state, and national issues?

Then, I asked myself this question. Given any aspiring minister inadequately trained, which type congregation would he prefer? Would he choose the informed or the well uniformed?

Ironically, we had two teachers and one counselor who worked with free public adult education, a day program and a night program.

Deacon Wills began to show his old age; his health started to decline.

Deacon Simpson began to assist Deacon Wills.

The deacon ministry increased during Rev. Jamison's tenure.

A young gentleman, who grew up in the church, and a much older man joined the spiritual leadership rank.

Eugene Allen and the now late Darell Grand's appointments pleased the membership. Of all the things Deacon Allen could have been doing, he chose church leadership.

During the 70's drugs infected Grand Rapids. Drugs touched almost every family, Black, Hispanic or White. Addicts killed citizens daily. Guess what? Addicts interrupted church worship services on Sundays at 11:00 a.m. with a bang, bang! "Give up the money or I'll blow your brains out!" Those hooked on heroin seized this chance to support their habits. Fortunately, God spared us the agony. Nevertheless, we had five break-ins. Once the robbers took an expensive Bible, the public-address system, and a gold cross.

By now the pastor and his wife began to enjoy their toddler. She had just turned four.

Pastor Jamison conducted a revival in Florida. He loved having this opportunity to preach for a week in that state. While there he told one of his Florida friends about his personal life. Unfortunately, someone with ties to Grand Rapids overheard his conversation.

"I am going to divorce my wife, Bobbi and marry another Bobbye in my congregation," Rev. Jamison responded.

Before Rev. Jamison returned home, the news preceded him.

Pastor Jamison was conducting a Bible class on *Marriage Counseling - Staying Together* before the Florida revival.

Weeks later after observing the pastor's action, the deacons confronted the pastor. But the pastor became defensive.

The deacons became concerned after the pastor's reaction. They hired a private detective to investigate. They knew if this saga were true, it would split the church.

"One day as I made my routine rounds driving around the church and into the parking lot, I noticed Bobbye Grass's vehicle parked on the campus. I decided to park one-fourth block from the church. When I arrived at the front, I unlocked the door with a key provided me. Walking lightly, I slipped off my shoes and eased downstairs in my black socks. Upon arrival I noticed the pastor's office door was slightly ajar. I heard noises familiar to sexual activity, but I did not jump to any conclusion. Then, I heard, 'Oh Rev. I love you,' in a sweet, light, passionate voice. When I saw a pair of male pants and ladies undergarments lying on the floor, I had seen enough. Later I glimpsed the couple in a chair moving in a rhythmic pattern only they could understand.

At that moment, I crept back upstairs, left the premises and wrote this report."

August 09, 1974

Signed *E.O.*, Official Investigator

"LET NO MAN DESPISE THY YOUTH; BUT BE THOU AN EXAMPLE OF THE BELIEVERS IN WORD, IN CONVERSATION, IN CHARITY, IN SPIRIT, IN FAITH, IN PURITY." (I Timothy 4:12)

A turning point evolved, July 1974, when the pastor and the Senior Choir toured the South: Scottsboro and Birmingham, Alabama, St. Louis, Missouri, East St. Louis, Illinois, Edwards, Natchez and Jackson, Mississippi, including a television appearance in Jackson. What fun!

The tour almost ended without confusion. Large crowds showed up for all our concerts except in Natchez. In fact, the church that had invited us, Pleasant Green Christian Living, decided to shut us out after our arrival. But, resourceful Pastor Jamison appealed to several of his minister buddies who pulled through for him. One church took care of the hospitable things such as social gatherings and meals. Another church allowed us to perform.

That Sunday evening, the host church, Belmont Christian Living, presented concert one from 7:00 p.m. to 10:00 p. m. and then we began our concert at 10:00 p.m. Why didn't we decline and express our gratitude to them that night? Instead, we performed to an indifferent, cold, tired, and ungrateful audience. Regardless, we did our best. Any hostility we felt probably was not directed toward us. We just happened to be the receivers.

As soon as we returned from our tour more news greeted us! Students began giving members who taught at various high schools, tidbits about our church leader.

"Your pastor ain't nothing," a student blurted out. "My brother sees him some place," she said. "I know what's going on! It's near 20th and Main Street," she went on to say. The teacher became angry! That teacher disciplined the student and asked her to leave the classroom for her loud outbursts.

Organizations functioned: Mission, Children's Choir, which I directed, Mother's Board, Youth Department, Senior Choir, Young Adult Choir, Deacon Board, Trustee Board, Deaconess, Usher Board, the Scholarship Ministry, which I chaired, and Sunday school musicians which I supervised and guided.

Some members showed concern when Rev. Jamison began to get sick often. When hospitalized, he requested to see a few officials. He accepted a few calls.

Besides the church officials, somehow Bobbye's name cleared the limited hospital visitation list. But the congregation loved Bobbye. She had gained respect. Parishioners appreciated her pleasant caring personality. Bobbye encouraged the high school graduates each year. She remembered birthdays. It seems she never forgot the sick and elderly.

Bobbye sought individual counseling or one-on-one counseling as it is sometimes called. She participated in the marriage study group the pastor had started too.

Rev. Jamison said during one of his group sessions on marriage, "Seek help if you need it. Don't be ashamed," he went on to say. "That is what the Bible says."

Church officials tried to keep abreast of situations that could affect the congregation or cause uproars.

Deacon Wills asked the pastor what he planned to do.

"My business is my business and not yours," replied Rev. Jamison.

That statement shocked the deacons. And they did not accept it. Since the pastor refused to discuss the situation, Deacon Wills knew what he had to do.

Chapter 9

March 13, 1975

When Rev. Jamison walked into the sanctuary up to the rostrum, took his seat behind the pulpit, Deacon Wills approached the microphone. He addressed the congregation with poise. Only Wills could have done this at that moment.

"Dear church family, I apologize for the interruption in our morning service. We negotiated a ninety-day buy-out contract with Rev. Jamison as the church directed us to do. He agreed to the terms. Further, he agreed not to appear today, but you see he failed to keep his promise. A good man can be trusted."

Then he turned to Rev. Jamison.

"Rev. Jamison, I beg of you, please leave now so we can proceed with our worship service."

Most members applauded Deacon Wills. However, I heard a few *Uh-uh-uh*!

Wills turned to Rev. Jamison a second time.

Surprisingly, Rev. Jamison got up from his seat behind the sacred lectern, mumbled a few words of unhappiness, as he walked down from the pulpit to the left aisle leading to the lower level which housed his office.

It appeared that this display of action had been planned.

Rev. Richards left the organ and joined his mentor, Rev. Jamison. Teresa Marshall, pianist, followed.

Maybe one or two other members left the choir loft. I can't remember exactly. But, everyone remembers Bobbye, her sister, Reeia Buckman, leaving the choir loft and Reeia's three teenagers joining as they walked down the aisle making their dramatic exit.

Willie Rose, wife of Richards, descended from the Senior Usher Board section, center back, and left too.

"I am sick and tired of certain people at this church spreading rumors about my sister going with Pastor Jamison," Reeia said at our last church meeting.

"It's not true; it's just not true," she went on to say. "It's a down right lie!" she yelled.

"My sister doesn't have anything to do with Mrs. Jamison and Pastor Jamison's love affair." Then she burst into tears and ran out the church door!

Almost everyone looked seemingly without empathetic eyes, and heard Reeia without sympathetic ears that Tuesday evening.

Perhaps eight, nine or ten others from the audience that Sunday joined in the protest parade.

Mrs. Jamison, the first lady, remained seated shaking her head as the walkout show progressed and ended.

The church went numb!

But no one spoke harsh words outwardly; no physical fights occurred. No violence or guns showed up in the sanctuary.

Time soon came for us to move on.

I thought…sweet spirit and Christian fellowship…kindred minds likened to Him above?

At that instance, I jumped up from my seat, went to the piano and began playing.

What a fellowship, what a joy divine….

Did the choir and church sing!

A church-like mood returned!

Chapter 10

December 10, 1984

Rev. Richardson could preach! He had members sitting on the edge waiting for the next word. Sometimes I thought I knew the exact word he might say next. On the contrary, he presented a more challenging thought my mind had not yet conceived.

This time the church elected a pastor and teacher, young, energetic and eager to become a church leader. However, his sermons came across as a ten-year veteran. His speaking voice itself demanded our attention and respect. Rev. Calvin Richardson grew up living with his grandmother and grandfather.

His grandfather had spiritual charge of a small family church in North Chicago, Illinois, where he groomed his grandson to become a preacher man.

"Preach boy preach!" his grandfather often said when he visited.

Granddaddy, Rev. Richardson called the elder, must have been in his late 80's.

Rev. Richardson, married with a daughter and son, had lots of preaching experience for a twenty-six year old. He practiced and developed his style while having relatives listen to him…grandparents, parents, siblings, nieces, nephews and some close friends.

Rev. Richardson had to overcome one obstacle…past participles! *Had did* took the place of *had done.*

The directress of Bible in Action, Lorene, spoke to him one day. She told him the concern a few members had voiced to her. Those concerned did not want the school children hearing incorrect past participles from the pulpit each Sunday morning.

This very bright pastor and teacher said, "Teach me." Other than that, he could a-r-t-i-c-u-l-a-t-e!

Actually, the lessons unbeknowingly came from someone else, but the directress taught them. The happy-go-lucky pastor mastered this previously missed skill in just two short lessons.

For the first time, we broadcasted live the 11:00 a.m. service by way of a local radio station.

The community fell in love with our leader's preaching style.

Soon we became the Grand Rapids, Michigan, household church.

Christmas of 1983, the Senior Choir sponsored an extravaganza with voices, drums, piano, keyboard, organ and strings. Besides the usual Christmas carols, the Senior Choir performed classics such as *Mary Had a Baby* by William Dawson and *Carol of the Bells by Peter J. Wilhousky.* Ronald, a high school senior that year, played the keyboard, which gave colorful background to the music. The keyboard had not been introduced to our congregation. Decorations stood out! The community filled the sanctuary. The Christmas music, old and new, lifted hearts.

With lights out and candles burning, the processional, consisting of singers dressed in bright red blouses and shirts and white skirts and pants, began. C.O.H. provided this special sacred service for the community.

Roberta and Selina, who planned the program, had no idea the outcome would be of such magnitude. This perhaps surpassed any church Christmas performance in our city's history.

The Scholarship ministry provided a great service for high school graduates. Although I chaired the group, Mrs. Simpson, Mrs. Myles, Deacon Harris, Trustee Carr, Mrs. Mary Johnson, and Mrs. McNair did the work.

That year the committee chose to have a fundraiser. The group sold blue and gold church tee shirts. The fifth Sunday's mission plate could never have produced large scholarships for that year's seniors.

What a smash! I enjoyed working with this group!

As a result of the tee shirt project, all twelve graduates received $1,000 just by submitting to the committee, a copy of an acceptance letter from a post-secondary training institution.

Ezell Fields, Harry Smith, and Michael Harris joined the spiritual leadership rank. Rev. Richardson appointed them to the Deacon Board.

C.O.H. lost a soldier! Deacon Wills slipped away forever.

Fred, the church young minister of music, founded a new choir called Harmony and Inspiration. It welcomed young adults somewhat younger than the members in the Senior Choir.

C.O.H. invited Rev. Jamison back for the twenty-third church anniversary.

Joe Savannah, the person who chaired the affair, has always identified with Rev. Jamison. He convinced the committee to extend the invitation. He and his nephew Charles still believe that the church wronged Rev. Jamison for dismissing him. Joe wanted to make things right.

At the end of the 11:00 a.m. church service that Sunday, Rev. Jamison asked to speak to the congregation. After all visitors left, except Rev. Jamison's wife Bobbye, he began to explain.

"C.O.H.," he said, "I am a changed man. I apologize if I did anything wrong before I left here. Will you accept my apology?" The church responded.

"Yes."

The quick meeting adjourned.

"Rev. Richardson, I clocked you driving 65 miles per hour in a 55 m.p.h. zone. I have to give you a ticket," said the officer according to our pastor.

"Yes sir," the Rev. reported he said to the officer.

The members loved Rev. Richardson and his disposition. The younger members could identify with him as well as the old ones. Our twenty-eight year old pastor looked to be forty. We believed the pastor loved our youth. He instituted meaningful activities for the Children's Choir, Jr. Usher Board, and the Youth Department...Bible bowls, field trips, socials or sockhops, bowling, cookouts, and retreats. The Youth Department established basketball teams for the church and community boys, even the 38-year-old *boys*. We had it going on!

Our annual gross income had reached nearly $300,000. We felt great!

A larger sister church began to invite Rev. Richardson to assist with their services. Their pastor, a Dearhouse College man, had grown in age. His health began to fail.

Rev. Frank John helped us when we needed it between pastors. We thought nothing of Rev. Richardson's assisting St. Jude. But when Rev. John died and Rev. Richardson kept on going, some members began to think about our future.

An associate preacher, Rev. William Milburn, led our church services.

It has not been a custom for Christian Living Baptist Church pastors to leave one church in a given city for a larger one in the same city, right down the street, with the same zip code, except when a church splits.

Did St. Jude want assistance or our pastor?

Regardless of the one hundred eighty thousand citizens in Grand Rapids, the Black religious circles all connect within families, friendships, employment and social groups.

Church secrets…forget it!

"Rev. Richardson, are you planning to resign and become pastor of St. Jude?" asked Roberta.

"No way," replied Rev. Richardson.

Roberta felt better for a short while.

Not only did Roberta ask that question; Sarah, Selina, Tracy, Darlene and Bobbie began to poll Rev. Richardson as well.

The ministry is no different than any other occupation, when it comes to family financial needs. I understood that, but I did not want to lose our dynamic preacher!

By December 31, 1984, our pastor resigned!

In a church meeting Molly Johns posed this question to Deacon Smith.

"Deacon Smith, will your new chairmanship add too much responsibility for you? Now, you chair the church's three highest level positions. Let's face it, you operate your own business."

"No, Mrs. Johns," said Deacon Smith. "I feel I can handle all jobs without any conflicts."

Smith surprised me wearing a small gold earring in his left ear.

Mrs. Johns, a social worker, knew all about power and what too much can do. She also knew a spouse needs to spend time with the family. All too often she has dealt with the outcome of parents failing to spend enough time with families, especially the children. In addition, she felt this question needed to be raised and recorded in the official church minutes.

Deacon Simpson, brother-in-law of Molly, spoke up.

"I am willing to work with the board in any way I can." Simpson commented.

"Let's face it, three demanding jobs given to one person in a church defies rationality," concluded Mrs. Johns.

In July the Senior Choir went on a mini tour. This time we chose the Capitol City, Washington, D.C. Two choir members had adult children living there, Darlene and Sarah.

What wonderful concerts, two of them! What great people!

The sad commentary we learned on our way home. Our young minister of music, Fred, did not walk away from an offer a D.C. church had made to him. But for Fred I guess he needed to move on.

Chapter 11

April 07, 1985

Easter Sunday service began on time. The church had hired Cecil Bell to replace Fred.

Pearl Sanders had been appointed to announce a church meeting.

"A church meeting will be held at 7:00 p.m. on Tuesday, April 18, 1985. Each member must be present. We plan to end the church mess," said Pearl.

"Is she trying to start something?" I overheard a choir member say.

We had clear procedures for church meetings.

Only the chairman of the deacon board could make the initial announcement, either verbally or written, when without a pastor. The first announcement had to be made at least two weeks before said date.

But as the service progressed, members learned the real reason Pearl made the announcement.

Pearl, a very outspoken, overly opinionated, petite dark lady had been given a spot during our a.m. worship service to speak to the membership about the court injunction.

Of course, visitors sat and listened.

Someone had found a copy of Pearl's notes of a secret meeting. Pearl and Harris had planned to use worship time to elicit support for the PC's actions.

Easter that year came the first Sunday in April.

Everyone anticipated the usual church ritual, the Lord's Supper. The Holy Communion has always been a monthly occurrence on first Sundays, most of the times, during the 11:00 a.m. services.

A shock came when Deacon Smith made this announcement.

"If Easter falls on a first Sunday, a Christian Living Baptist Church should not partake the Lord's Supper." He refused to provide communion on that day.

Smith claimed he had just become intelligent about this concept. Man makes a lot of discoveries. But I don't think this one had any credibility. The real reason…Smith needed the time.

After the former minister of music, Rev. Richards, preached, "Can You Mess with That?" Pearl took the microphone.

Pearl's assignment…preach to the plaintiffs and continue a brainwashing job the church leaders began with the rest of the membership.

"DARE ANY ONE OF YOU, HAVING A MATTER AGAINST ANOTHER, GO TO THE LAW BEFORE THE UNJUST AND NOT BEFORE THE SAINTS? DO YE NOT KNOW THAT THE SAINTS WILL JUDGE THE WORLD? AND IF THE WORLD SHALL BE JUDGED BY YOU, ARE YOU UNWORTHY TO JUDGE THE SMALLEST MATTERS?" (I Corinthians 6:1-2)

"Don't take your Christian brother to court," Pearl went on to say quite strongly.

She failed, however, to define Christian brother, or identify one's Christian brothers.

Well, I sang in the choir, but I had heard enough!

Pearl and the church officials loved quoting scriptures. However, no one quoted this one:

"WHEREFORE THE LORD SAID, FORASMUCH AS THIS PEOPLE DRAW NEAR ME WITH THEIR MOUTH, AND WITH THEIR LIPS DO HONOUR ME, BUT HAVE REMOVED THEIR HEART FAR FROM ME, AND THEIR FEAR TOWARD ME IS TAUGHT BY THE PRECEPT OF MEN." (Isaiah 29:13)

I delighted myself in leaving with my husband, Trustee Walton, Ronald, and niece Delphine.

No plaintiff had a chance for rebuttal and it would have been just as out of place. Members left home for a spiritual service, not an Easter Sunday church meeting.

About fifteen others excused themselves and walked out.

Our exit said, *excuse us; we don't have to hear this today*!

The thing that bothered me…several college students, home for Easter, looked forward to taking the sacrament and participating in our monthly fellowship.

Instead, this change forced our college students to listen to propaganda.

"This is God's house! You may win in court, but you can't win in God's house," Pearl sarcastically uttered as I departed.

When members learned of the injunction, the two divisions became bitterly pronounced. Those who voted for Rev. Jamison gnawed at those who did not. Some who voted for Rev. Clark fought back.

After the injunction documents had been served, Deacon Smith announced the following Sunday:

"Church, I have some sad news to report! Some members have sued C.O.H! A state trooper delivered the papers to us."

Smith managed to get about half the members in attendance to believe every word he said.

He then began: "Deacon Bernard Simpson, Deacon Jack Savannah, Deacon Ezell Fields, Sister Roberta Jones, Sister Molly Johns, Trustee Randall Stove, Trustee Howard Morner, Trustee Andy Robinson and Trustee Thomas Walton."

I did not attend church that Sunday morning and did not hear Smith's theatrical production. That day my sisters and I performed a $10,000 benefit concert for the Dr. Erin Myles Scholarship fund.

But I learned after Smith's remarks, hostility increased between the two factions.

Chapter 12

August 23, 1985

"What is the woman's role in our church?" Selina asked in a church meeting. That profound question remains unanswered.

In the initial stages without a pastor and a change in chairman of the deacon board, the church functioned seemingly well.

The PC set up a plan to follow based on the church's constitution. Visiting speakers preached during the 11:00 a.m. service. Members voiced their opinions by writing comments.

A few ministers came just to deliver a sermon and enjoy a free trip.

Some seemed worthy of consideration. Somehow, I still felt our leadership used unfair screening criteria....

Concerned female members watched carefully, including me. Several females had volunteered to serve on the PC. I wanted input, but I had no ambitions to serve on the committee.

Deacon Harris, a bald headed gentleman, spoke forcefully against women serving on the PC or assisting in any way. Harris, like Deacon Smith, had moved up through the ranks rather quickly. He weighed about one hundred twenty-pounds, and appeared to believe what he preached. "Women should not be in the pulpit, serve as a deacon, be a member of the pulpit committee or lead the church's Christian education training programs," he often said.

Frankly, most members did not know either of these men too well. Everyone knew they belonged to our church, both were intelligent, held good jobs they trained themselves to acquire. Harris had a wife and six children.

No one could be quite sure about the status of Smith's family. The female who claimed to have been his wife disappeared with two children, never to be heard from again. Mrs. Johns had been misinformed about his family status. Smith now has a live-in friend. He has been accused of impregnating a single mother in our congregation. True or

41

not, if this involved anyone else, Smith and Harris certainly would have quoted:

"LET THE DEACONS BE THE HUSBANDS OF ONE WIFE, RULING THEIR CHILDREN AND THEIR OWN HOUSES WELL." (I Timothy 3:12)

At any rate, Smith and Harris, chairman and vice-chairman of the PC, led the church. The leadership, most plaintiffs felt, came from Harris rather than Smith, but Smith informed us.

Another rather young gentleman, Deacon Allen, once well respected, had assumed the secretary's position. Deacon Allen, married with three respected college sons, had been around for a while. One son sang with the Harmony and Inspirationals. He expressed a desire to unite with St. Jude, but Dad kept the family together.

A guest minister, Rev. David Matthews, moved the congregation. A deep thinker, young, gifted, and intelligent, he could have led us well during the 21st century.

Unfortunately, Deacon Harris knew Rev. Matthews. For some unknown reason, Harris had developed a dislike for Rev. Matthews. Harris never moved an eyebrow when Matthews spoke. Harris, being a strong voice among the less affluent members of the board and congregation, triumphed. Rev. Matthews never had a bit of a chance. Members knew this *kid*. Three of his former high school teachers, a counselor, and four neighbors knew his character. Now, he pastors a major church in New Chicago, Indiana.

<u>Official Ballot</u>

(Circle One)

1. Jamison, Leroy
2. Coleman, Samuel
3. Dumas, Willis
4. None of the above

This ballot indicated the PC abandoned fairness, the church constitution and *Robert's Rules of Order*.

Even with the unfair advantage given Rev. Jamison by placing his name in the number one spot, he could not muster up the 55% required votes. We went back to square one.

On the first try to elect a pastor, a large number of members expressed concerns; we all agreed to go home without casting any votes, think about what we had to do with a more serious outlook. No doubt this gave the PC more time to strategize.

Members continued to complete the visiting minister request form. Requests kept coming for Matthews again and again.

Rev. Matthews did return. It appeared the church had made a decision. The membership wanted Matthews!

Later, when a third attempt to elect a pastor occurred, the congregation demanded the names be placed on the ballot alphabetically using *Robert's Rules of Order*.

This time Smith and Harris decided Matthews would give difficult competition. At the last minute, the PC removed Matthews' name from a prepared ballot and created a new one. Somehow the scheme to sneak Rev. Sam Clark's name on the ballot leaked. He had received the third highest number of requests.

As a result, an informed member sent church voters biographical information about the new second choice candidate. I received that information. It looked pretty darn good to me.

In an earlier meeting, the membership agreed to place only two names on the ballot.

Rev. Jamison lost again!

Deacon Barnes, Deacon Johnson and several other deacons wept unbelievably at the end of the church meeting.

Barnes said, "I'm leaving this old church."

The PC couldn't take it.

On that December evening, Smith and Harris began a long campaign of maneuvers to overturn the election. They excluded

Simpson, the two Savannah brothers and Fields from their contemptuous plan.

"Unfortunately, our church morale has sunk to an all time low," remarked Simpson.

"The top Christian leaders have begun Satan-like acts," Deacon Fields replied.

Several church members were informed that defendants had a connection to the underground world. The telephone informant, who refused to identify himself or the church official, called two plaintiffs. The anonymous tipster commented that certain churchgoers had better watch their backs. Further the tipster said, a *tidy sum* had been delivered to one church official. The source warned, "Be careful: they can't lose!" I didn't know what to believe! In an era of drugs and killings, this frightened plaintiffs and plaintiff supporters too.

August 1985 C.O.H. learned the meaning of how the Lord giveth and how the Lord taketh.

Heaven received four of our best:

1) *Mary Johnson*, August 15, 1985, 75, a retired registered nurse, wife of Deacon Johnson, died from a rare degenerative bone disease.
2) *Ida Bulwark*, August 19, 1985, 80, choir member, young senior citizen at heart, succumbed to a heart attack.
3) *Bernice Starks*, August 20, 1985, 40, mother of three teens, daughter of Mrs. Lauren Wilson, step-daughter of Deacon Wilson, lost her courageous battle with cancer.
4) Finally, August 23, 1985, *Erin Myles, Pharm. D.,* 24, daughter of Melvin and Darlene Myles, niece of Roberta and Lorene, niece and goddaughter of Thomas and me, left us too. A wrongful Illinois toll road car accident claimed the life of this young member.

Chapter 13

April 09, 1986

"Hear ye, hear ye…this court will now come to order with Judge Stewart presiding," announced the bailiff.

Plaintiffs who represented the 55% felt that this court appearance would reveal the whole truth.

The plaintiff supporters wore to court church tee shirts which symbolized love and concern. Thirty-five plaintiff supporters showed up. It shocked us to observe no defendant spectators came. That seemed weird! Later, we suspected two persons attending wearing tee shirts who sat with the plaintiff supporters actually rallied for the defendants.

The judge announced that she would meet with the attorneys and church leaders in a private session and return to inform the court of her decisions.

Everyone visited as we waited for answers from the judge. We felt good and had faith in the American court system that justice would surely be served.

When the private session ended, about two hours later, the judge made the following announcement:

"Lawyers will hold briefings with their clients in the library, a large room down the hall from my chambers. I will reschedule in about ten days. I want to end this dispute as soon as possible."

The motor in my mind ran at full speed. I had never experienced a civil court session.

"This court is adjourned," the judge said.

The court system has a great significance for many people, especially for Blacks. However, down through the years in my community, I often heard that Black on Black cases have less weight than other cases, and judges fear church disputes.

I really didn't know. I watched everything. I attended the court session to see for myself.

Both sides gathered in the library; defendants sat on the left and plaintiffs on the right.

All leaders agreed with the following plan:

1. *That two persons would represent each side*
2. *That the two attorneys and four leaders would set a date to meet*
3. *That they would create and propose a plan to end the dispute*
4. *That the attorneys would notify the judge about the agreed plan*
5. *That each side would select a non-partisan person to represent the group*
6. *That the four leaders would agree on one person to work with both sides*

Deacon Johnson decided to leave his group to sit with the plaintiffs. Deacon Johnson said, "What y'all doing? We know what's going on. You can't win anyway."

A plaintiff supporter informed Attorney Brown. Attorney Brown asked Johnson to leave and follow the directions set forth by the judge. The plaintiffs and their supporters watched carefully.

Deacon Wilson had accused the plaintiff supporters of inappropriate behavior. He said poor behavior forced the PC to withhold information from the congregation. Somehow poor behavior to Deacon Wilson meant not accepting what the PC forced on us.

Chapter 14

May 05, 1986

"Oh God, I don't believe you said that!" cried Diana. She saw the blasphemy.

On the first Sunday, May 05, 1986, Deacon Smith announced to the congregation that he had decided to change the order of the Holy Communion. Instead of the usual ceremony where the deacons in charge assist the minister with the distribution of the bread, which represents the broken body of Christ, and wine, which symbolizes the blood of Christ, Smith decided to discontinue the deacons' services. He felt the church's dispute gave him the authority to choose to withdraw their services. A **you-come-and-get-it-if-you-want-to** style replaced our tradition.

That irritated Smith's supporters as well as the plaintiffs and their supporters. The Christian Living Baptist Church does not play with the Holy Communion! However, on the first try, the visiting minister, Rev. Elijah Jones, rejected the decision for a change.

Instead, the minister told Smith, "I will adhere to the regular order of service."

Smith and Harris refused to cooperate. Smith caused dissention within his own camp. The other fellow deacons split right down the middle on this one.

The next communion Sunday, Smith's plan prevailed. However, I still cared about the church and hoped it would remain a traditional Christian Living Baptist Church.

News hit our congregation that one of our inactive members, Sally, known as a person in need of services, went to St. Jude to visit her former pastor. This particular Sunday, Rev. Richardson had invited several of his leading Chicago minister friends to his church. After service they feasted in the lower level of the church. Sally joined the group for lunch. She had just given birth to a baby boy about a week earlier.

As the group fellowshipped, Sally yelled, "My pussy hurts."

Several people sitting near her tried to play it off and tried to get her to stop this loud outburst. One mother of the church went over and suggested peace, please. Sally got louder saying the same thing again, "My pussy does hurt! I ought to know!"

Somehow the fried chicken, collard greens, potato salad and cornbread took on another taste…embarrassment!

Rev. Richardson, so taken by the display of this behavior, suddenly got up and went to his office.

Meanwhile, when Rev. Richardson returned and gave remarks, he said, "Let us continue to pray for drug addicts all over the country, those in your family, my family, your church, my church and those in no church or no family!"

He had said it all!

Chapter 15

June 03, 1986

C.O.H. still functioned with all departments operating partially. But, some members on both sides began to give less than their best...disgusted! What started as an invisible disagreement had now turned into tangible happenings right before each member's eyes.

A few members who gave their support to the PC said they just wanted a pastor.

Deacon Wilson prayed an oral prayer during one Sunday worship service.

"Lord, I don't care who you send for our pastor. I'll follow a cat if you send one!"

Wilson, who is the oldest deacon, has very light brown skin, stands six feet tall and weighs two hundred fifty pounds. He had just made his sixty-fifth birthday. As a young man and old one too, he has enjoyed slicked-back jet-black hair. With his consistency, no one knows what aids him. However, one might suspect Mrs. Clairol. For a long time he remained a widower. His first wife had served the church well many years before God called her home. While single about ten years ago, he dated two ladies in our congregation who sat near each other on Sundays and Wednesday nights. One Wednesday night at prayer meeting that caused a problem for him. The pastor, then Rev. Richardson, had to separate the two church sisters who fought childishly over their lover. Then, the pastor had to counsel the parties about their roles in the entanglement and about the role of mature Christians.

Deacon Wilson had been a dutiful church officer before his hands and neck began to give him health problems.

By now the nine plaintiffs and others who followed them had begun to plan new strategies. The leaders tried to keep followers abreast of court related actions with private meetings.

Defendants allowed plaintiffs and their supporters, at any service, to read scriptures, pray or sing songs with the choir and the audience.

An ugly profile had shown its face. That disturbed me!

Court ordered guidelines revealed the following:

1. *No church gatherings of any kind could be held to discuss or make plans about the conflict unless approved by the court.*
2. *The court would agree on a church meeting date.*
3. *Voting would be carried out through secret ballots.*
4. *A court-approved moderator would preside.*

By the time we learned about this plan, the defendants had decided to do their own thing again.

Deacon Smith called a mandatory meeting of the Soldiers' Council. The Soldiers' Council consists of all the deacons, trustees, and chairpersons of all organizations or ministries.

Most of us in attendance expressed our feelings. I told the DB my innermost feelings. I bluntly stated that I had respected them for twenty-five years. But the respect ended with their mistreatment.

"Deacons, you abused and misused us. You even lied and cheated. You overruled an official church decision for a pastor and hired your choice. Now you expect us to accept your overthrow, respect your leadership, and pay the salary for your choice. How stupid do you think we are? I like each of you as a person, but I surely hate your irresponsible behavior."

You should have seen the guilty look in their eyes.

Then I took my seat. Of course what I said shocked them, but they kept their stance, as I expected. However, I knew the fire burned in their consciences.

On June 3rd Smith again defied court orders and held a church meeting. The entire membership attended; that proved a big mistake for the plaintiffs. The plaintiff leaders misjudged the significance of attending, rejecting the idea of some supporters who recommended sitting this one out.

That evening at 6:30 p.m., Smith became afraid; so he said. The tears appeared real. Smith stated, "I cannot preside at this meeting," in a breaking voice with big tears on his pale face. "The judge said if I do, I'll be in contempt." A loud voice from the back said, "Why the hell did you schedule the meeting?"

Smith did not answer the unknown voice. Instead he said, " I have asked Francis Carr, the church clerk, to preside."

Francis, talented, competitive and aggressive, took the chair proudly! This power intrigued her. Everyone expected surprises! And surprises we got!

At the meeting, like worship services, plaintiffs or plaintiff supporters had no roles except voting on issues.

Before the vote, Trustee Morner asked to discuss an issue, but the chair declined any discussion. The trustee rose to tell a story. Morner grew angry! According to him, I learned later, Morner wanted to tell what happened to his son in the church basement during the 70's. The chair refused to let Trustee Morner speak because she knew about the decade-old incident.

Mrs. Carr then said, "All for Rev. Leroy Jamison please stand."

Deacon Harris and Francis controlled the **unofficial** vote counting.

Once when they called for votes for those objecting Jamison to stand, Mrs. Carr counted three people near me as one. She said "**18, 18,** and **18.**" It should have been **18, 19,** and **20.**

What a long subjectively conducted meeting! In another instance while Harris counted a lady Smith had dated, he skipped over her and went to the next person. For example, Smith's used-to-be-girlfriend should have been 40. He skipped her and gave the person next to her number 40. That person should have been 41. But the used-to-be- girlfriend, a verbal, intelligent lady, spoke loudly and diffused his plan. Well, about ten plaintiff supporters became frustrated with recounting. So, after the third attempt, they left.

During the course of the meeting, the church clerk approved a youngster's voting privilege who had not yet turned nine. His parents, defendant supporters and Mrs. Carr, wanted that vote to count regardless of the constitution's age requirement.

After four attempts of counting the votes, the chair proudly announced, "52 for and 51 against. Rev. Leroy Jamison now pastors C.O.H."

Attorney James Blair, the defendants' lawyer, suddenly quit! We learned he refused to work with a group of *Christians* who could not follow his legal advice or the judge's orders. The plaintiffs saluted Attorney Blair.

The defendants paid Attorney Blair right from the church treasury and hired another attorney.

The injunction still barred Rev. Jamison from the pulpit.

Deacon Smith announced the next Sunday, " Rev. Jamison won the election and now pastors C.O.H."

Area churches, especially those pastors who befriended Rev. Jamison, began making announcements too.

Deacon Johnson tried to get out of testifying in court. His brother, Trustee Johnson, a retired carpenter, handled the scheme. Strange happenings began to occur! Trustee Johnson met with Attorney Brown. Gossip had leaked at the church about Johnson's visit with Lawyer Brown.

One plaintiff supporter overheard a defendant supporter using the word *payoff* before church service one Sunday. That defendant supporter went on to say, "We don't have to worry about anything." Finally, the member said, "Thank you. Thank you, Jesus." That plaintiff supporter who overheard the secret conversation did not understand what those dingy statements meant.

Smith, Harris and Rev. Jamison met with the church secretary.

"Mrs. Floyd, we need to downsize," stated Harris.

"Sorry, we need to dismiss you," Smith eased out.

The plaintiffs and their supporters knew the scoop. The defendants wanted the secretary to be down and outside of the business.

On the next court date Attorney Brown explained to the plaintiffs in her session with us that Trustee Johnson had indeed visited her office.

"He and I have ties; we are second cousins. He requested a favor. He asked me not to put his brother on the stand to testify. I promised him I would not. His brother has health problems," Attorney Brown proclaimed!

No one said a word!

Chapter 16

June 11, 1986

Darlene and I always made the arrangements for the meetings, calling all persons we felt who wanted to be in the know. In doing so, we soon became skeptical of several persons who appeared each time without a call. Yet, we wondered, if we did not call, how did they know about our meetings?

Deacon Simpson and Deacon Fields conducted the meeting at the Douglas Library.

I often assisted in the devotional services with a favorite hymn, *Yield Not to Temptation or Where He Leads*. The piano put some **oomph** in our meeting.

"Let's have a prayer sit-in," suggested Trustee Walton. "Think about it. Who can criticize a prayer meeting? Pray for the good, pray for the bad, pray for the cheater, liar and pray for the ones who make decisions in our church, city, state and federal government. They all need lots of prayer."

Deacon Simpson and Deacon Fields nodded for another speaker to talk.

"Ask to speak to the congregation. Almost no one on the opposite side has heard our position. They have been told to ignore our newsletters," I uttered.

"Let's meet in our church rather than this library!" Trustee Walton cried out.

Lawyer Brown gave no help in this matter. When confronted that Deacon Smith used brainwashing techniques for senior citizens during the eleven o'clock worship service and during all other department meetings, Attorney Brown replied, "So!"

"Our meetings should be held in our church. It's easy to move out, but it's harder to move back in. What can anyone say? Defendants are using our money to pay their lawyers. We are paying our own way. Besides, C.O.H. belongs to us too," Walton reiterated.

Fields and Simpson placed their emphasis on following the court guidelines and privacy.

Tracy rang out, "Why can't we do something differently? We have the expertise right here."

"Confront the defendants!" suggested Roberta. "All people do not learn at the same rate. Ask pre-planned questions to help them understand the magnitude of what they did."

By now things for us had begun to take a different turn. I hoped for a turn-around, but some doubts began to set in my mind. "If we don't change our plan of action, we will give them the case," I said.

I remembered Trustee Johnson's visit to Attorney Brown. I remembered the Soldiers' Council meeting. I remembered the unofficial church meeting. I remembered the defendants' lawyer quit. I remembered how Smith allowed Pearl to reprimand the plaintiffs on Easter Sunday. I remembered how the PC called secret meetings with invited participants. I remembered how Smith misled the congregation saying nine members had sued the church. I remembered how the officials refused to follow court orders. I remembered that Rev. Jamison and the deacons had fired the secretary. I remembered that the deacons had given Rev. Jamison a contract. I concluded...the defendants have a proactive plan.

I couldn't forget Deacon Harris's position on splitting the church. I couldn't forget how Deacon Smith refused to communicate with us. Plenty of concerns I couldn't forget!

I had a lot to chew, digest and swallow.

Defendant supporters became quite creative. They used cash from offerings to pay Rev. Jamison. A few ladies chose to write Rev. Jamison a check directly, instead of writing their checks to the church. Who could question that?

"Do everything in a Christlike manner," Fields and Simpson continued to say.

Frankly, the plaintiff supporters grew weary. Some of us knew faith without smart planning and work is dead.

Biological brothers, Deacons E. Savannah and J. Savannah expressed themselves, but they never conflicted with Simpson and Fields.

In the meantime, back at church, we hungered for inspiration and guidance, comfort in sorrow, help with living in a mean world of chaos and emptiness. Despite that, we kept on going.

One week about thirty of us attended the weekly Bible study. Christian Living founders would have been proud of us. That night we discussed *Religious Leadership*. No one could deny us a voice there. However, only about fifteen defendants and their supporters participated that week.

As we discussed our history, we showed unity. But as soon as anyone connected the Whites mistreating Blacks in the past, with our Black leaders mistreating and abusing other Blacks in our churches, the defendants could not understand. In otherwords, discussing Whites abusing our people during slavery or even now made sense to them. It proved too painful for the defendants and their supporters to talk about Black on Black mistreatment and abuse, especially in our churches.

At one of the plaintiff's meetings, we talked about staying together and the importance of it. Actually, we had been a very vital core of the services. We provided finance, know-how, availability, and numbers. You name it...without us things would certainly be different.

Plaintiffs and their supporters decided to decrease their giving to five dollars per adult per Sunday. We captured the attention of the defendants, their supporters, and their packets too!

Chapter 17

June 13, 1986

Can you believe it? Another day in court finally came, June 13th.
Soon after the plaintiffs arrived, a few defendants showed up.

Lawyer Brown and Judge Stewart decided to postpone the session. The reason...Lawyer Campbell had gone to a workshop in Mississippi.

Deacon Smith did not appear.

Why hadn't Lawyer Brown informed us about the postponement?

By now Rev. Jamison had begun to participate in more church activities.

He taught a Bible class during Vacation Bible School. He began attending Sunday school teachers' meetings. The following Sunday he assisted with serving communion.

Rev. Jamison hated Smith's communion arrangement. Therefore, the next Sunday, Deacon Smith announced, "We will return to our regular tradition for serving communion." Before this incident, other than having problems with the word *supper,* officials had kept a reasonable order of serving the Holy Communion. On the contrary, they have not decided if taking the Lord's Supper during the day represents the same symbolism as it does taking it at night. Rev. Jamison, too, believes it's a *SUPPER* not a *DINNER*!

The official board still used money from the church's treasury to pay for their personal legal defense. This time Smith wrote a $15,000 check. Rev. Jamison's name appeared on the church bulletin as pastor of the church. Had the defendants made a joke of the Grand Rapids Civil Court?

Rev. Jamison, also, received a check for $3,200 supposedly for retroactive pay.

The church leaders paid Rev. Jamison for moving his belongings to our church parsonage.

Attorney Brown told the plaintiffs and their supporters in our first meeting that she knew how to end the conflict quickly.

We all wanted to know her answer.

She replied, "If Rev. Clark decides to come, there will be no need for an injunction."

Deacon Simpson spoke up. "I talked to Rev. Clark myself and this is what Rev. Clark said."

"I will not begin to pastor a congregation with church leaders who have no regard for sound rules, by-laws, the Bible, or their fellow members. My desire is to pastor a church, not lead a cult."

Chapter 18

June 30, 1986

Nine plaintiffs and fifteen supporters showed up for the court session; the twelve defendants appeared, but still none of their supporters came to witness.

The bailiff called Judge Stewart's court to order. But after that....

Deacon Smith took the witness stand. Lawyer Brown asked him about violations which he carried out at a Soldiers' Council meeting and a church meeting.

Smith at first did not know about any violations. Lawyer Brown then began the specifics.

"Did you announce to the church that Rev. Jamison became pastor of C.O.H. on...?"

"Yes," Smith replied.

"Mr. Smith, did you know about the agreement both parties had made when you scheduled a church meeting?"

"No, I forgot."

"One more question, Mr. Smith, did you recall that the two-party agreement had been approved by Judge Stewart?"

"I did not read all the legal documents, therefore, I did not know," answered Deacon Smith.

Attorney Campbell cross-examined Smith. Campbell wanted to know how the conflict had affected the church.

"The plaintiffs and their supporters don't give much anymore. They used to give a lot. Needless to say, the finances dropped about 50%."

Plaintiff supporters in the audience just looked at each other.

"The court calls Michael Harris," Judge Stewart announced.

Harris gave his address, "101 Clay Road, Grand Rapids, Michigan."

"Are you an attorney?"

"I have both B. A. and M. S. degrees, but, I am not a lawyer," Harris indicated.

"Can you remember, Mr. Harris, that...?" Whatever Attorney Brown asked, Harris just could not remember. One thing for sure, Harris showed self-confidence. A few minutes later the judge called Rev. Leroy Jamison. "Reverend, did you receive a large check from C.O.H....on?" inquired Attorney Brown. Rev. Jamison said, "Yes, I did."

"Who wrote that check?" asked the lawyer.

"I have no idea!" replied the Reverend.

"Did you serve as Pastor after June 3rd...?" asked Attorney Brown.

"I did," replied Rev. Jamison. "Church officials informed me that a majority of the members voted for me in a church meeting. Therefore, I became pastor of the church."

"When you stated the church officials informed you, can you name an official?" asked the attorney.

"By that I meant Deacon Smith, chairman of the Pulpit Committee. Later he told me I was no longer pastor."

"Rev. Jamison, do you have a reserved parking space at C.O.H. marked, parking only for the pastor, Rev. Leroy Jamison, Sr.?"

"No."

"Are you living in the church parsonage?"

"No," in a loud voice, Rev. Jamison answered. "I live with a friend in Lake Park."

"Do you have any personal effects in the parsonage?"

"No, oh yes, I do have a computer, toolbox, water sprinkler, a calculator. That's all I have there."

The judge did suggest it seemed Rev. Jamison had moved in.

Rev. Jamison, Deacon Smith and Deacon Harris's testimonies conflicted with the facts. The plaintiffs began clearing throats. Once Judge Stewart did remind Deacon Smith that he swore to tell the truth.

No plaintiff' testified.

Attorney Campbell told the court that day, "In an injunction only the accused testifies."

I did wonder how the court could determine if those who testified told the truth.

The judge presided over an a.m. and a p.m. session. She informed us that she needed to call the witnesses again to clear up testimonies. She then dismissed the court.

Within the next few weeks, Deacon Smith announced to the congregation, "The Grand Rapids Civil Court has scheduled a church meeting on October 15, 1986."

According to Smith, Judge Stewart set these stipulations:

1) *No absentee ballots*
2) *Only secret ballots*
3) *One court approved moderator*

Deacon Simpson, Trustee Walton and Trustee Stove, his wife Darlene and I, met with Attorney Brown. "What happened, Lawyer Brown?" asked Trustee Walton.

"To be frank, I forgot to file a document with the judge," replied Attorney Brown.

"You got to be kidding!" I said to Attorney Brown.

At that moment, my mind began putting together small pieces of a large complicated puzzle.

Grand Rapids News ran an article on October 14th about Rev. William Wilkins, President, National Christian Living Baptist Convention, who resigned from his post because of criminal and immoral reasons. A judge in Arkansas sentenced him to sixteen years in prison without parole.

Chapter 19

October 15, 1986

What a crowd! People came from everywhere. Some probably had not been inside of C.O.H in years, except for weddings and funerals.

"Will you look at all these **CHURCH FOLK**?" Trustee Walton exclaimed as we entered the parking lot.

The deacons, all twelve, assembled up front for the usual prayer, scripture and song. But shortly after the togetherness, each went his separate way. I had a feeling that this might be the end of this deacon board.

The court approved moderator and leaders emerged from the audience. Leaders in charge of the meeting included: Deacon Clarence Moffett, Second Baptist Church, the plaintiff selected; Rev. Joe Jefferson, pastor, On The Cross Baptist Church, the defendants selected; and Rev. Robert Burgess, pastor, Good Grace Baptist Church. Both sides had agreed that Rev. Jefferson, who looked to be about fifty, would preside. The elder had very dark brown skin, and big eyes. He wore a black suit and white shirt, black socks and shoes. He even had on black tinted eyeglasses. He took charge! He knew he controlled the group. I could tell by the way he walked to the podium and I could tell by his voice inflectional variations.

"Good evening Christian friends," he said.

Rev. Jefferson gave the rules as he went along. No one questioned him. He spoke with authority to show he had been sanctioned by Grand Rapids' Civil Court.

"You must follow my direction if you want your vote counted," Rev. Jefferson blurted.

By now Rev. Jefferson had begun to develop his game plan.

Rev. Jefferson used to work for a local Grand Rapids firm alongside some of our church members years before this church injunction.

One day he told a friend, "There must be an easier way to make a living."

Well, he found a different way. He became a preacher and later a pastor of a church which he expanded.

The packed C.O.H. responded to Rev. Jefferson's directions. No leader from the plaintiffs' side voiced complaints. Of course no defendant objected.

Deacon Moffett spoke not a word. Plaintiff supporters wondered how could a quiet, almost timid acting, individual represent us well?

The Stoves and the Waltons had assisted in verifying the official church roster.

As Rev. Jefferson called each member's name, the person reported to the front of the church to receive his or her ballot.

However, shortly after I arrived I knew what confronted us.

Rev. Jefferson instructed us to circle the statement rejecting the Pulpit Committee's action or circle the statement accepting it.

Not all members understood what this was all about. Frankly, some voters did not care.

Some wanted to vote, get their fifty dollars and go home.

The members knew, "An inactive member is one who does not attend the church on a regular basis or does not contribute to the financial operation of the church."

One member challenged the moderator when he required participants to sign their *secret ballots*. Again, all church leaders remained silent, defendants and plaintiffs.

The plaintiff supporters anticipated signing a register.

When Dorea Brown questioned Rev. Jefferson about his procedures, the moderator flatly said, "If you don't sign your ballot as I directed you to do, I will see to it that your ballot is not counted. In fact, I'll put it in the waste basket myself."

Dorea did not sign her ballot. Rev. Jefferson said, "Now do you believe me?" as he placed it in a special basket.

I hated to see that! I knew with all the folks in attendance, the defendants would walk away with the largest number of votes.

But when the moderator called for a young boy's vote, I raised a question about age requirement. I approached the moderator with a paraphrase from the by-laws. "A child cannot vote until his 10th birthday." The boy in question had just turned nine. Although Mrs. Carr certified him to vote in the June church meeting, making the vote 51 – 52, Rev. Jefferson respected the bylaws.

"The plaintiffs **88** and the defendants **98**, announced Rev. Jefferson. This meeting is adjourned."

Chapter 20

October 17, 1986

Rev. Leroy Jamison, the new pastor, called a meeting of the Joint Board, October 17th.

Four deacon board members and four trustee board members, all plaintiffs, attended that meeting along with the rest of the church leadership.

During that meeting the defendants shouted, "**Jubilee! Jubilee!**"

Trustee Carr yelled, "Let's silence them."

"Yes, let's get rid of them," Deacon Harris spat out.

Rev. Jamison spoke up. "Now let's just end this here, tonight, letting by-gones be by-gones. Our goal...do the best for the church."

Deacons Simpson, E. Savannah, J. Savannah and E. Fields all agreed, that statement coming from Rev. Jamison helped to calm the rugged scene.

Trustees Walton, Stove, Morner, and McNair felt Rev. Jamison showed Christian leadership during that meeting.

After some emotional name calling, finger pointing, and mumbling from Carr and Harris about taking your Christian brothers to court, the first meeting adjourned with a bit of peace *and a* move-on *atmosphere.*

Third Sunday in October became known as *Happy Sunday* for those who chose the pastor they wanted.

For others, it had a different meaning. The church would never be the same.

I attended that third Sunday. What an experience of shouting, and plain old, frantic-like jumping around in the sanctuary. Those who went into a dance-frenzy produced a musty smell. The crowd, few in number, displayed a new spirit as they prayed, clapped, stomped and groaned, thanking God.

Two deacons testified.

Deacon Smith rose from his seat and walked to the podium. Every eye in the house watched his slightest move. He almost tripped over something. Not a word or a sigh!

"Church, I am so happy; I am moved! God is real to me. I am sorry if I did not carry out my duties as an official of this great church. The one thing I regret doing was changing the order of the Lord's Supper. Thank you Jesus for saving me." He went to his seat.

Rev. Jamison jumped up from his seat, center rostrum, "All y'all who forgive Deacon Smith, please stand."

Most of the members who attended church that day stood. I stood too.

The I-don't-care-if-the-church-splits deacon stood. He went to the microphone too, to ask for forgiveness.

"To my church family, I stand before you, today, to let you know I feel good. I need to thank those who supported me personally and those who voted for the deacons. Maybe I didn't keep my spiritual responsibilities as a deacon, but if I had to do it again, I would do everything exactly the same.

I stand by what I did as a deacon and what the Pulpit Committee did. I know I am a born again Christian. I told Trustee Walton in a meeting I would split the church for what I wanted, and we got it! Thank you again for supporting me," said Harris.

Again, Rev. Jamison rose to his feet and said, "All that accept Deacon Harris's apology, please stand."

This time the congregation seemed confused. Some stood. On the other hand, a majority of the members kept their seats.

My sister Lorene, who voted to accept the deacons' **mess** as she called it herself, remained seated.

My seat remained lukewarm! God knows I could not sanction that!

The court had not cleared Rev. Jamison for our church leader, so his buddy, Rev. Johnny Moorelest, preached. Rev. Moorelest had just completed a court required probationary period and counseling. He had been the pastor of a local church, City Road, where several members pressed charges against him for improper contact with their minor sons.

It didn't matter what Rev. Moorelest preached. I could predict what he would say on any given subject. He loved to dabble with the fire and brimstone sermons.

Several choir members complained about a strong offensive whiskey smell coming from the direction of the pulpit. I felt sorry about that.

Did Smith ever make an announcement saying the court had cleared Rev. Jamison? I don't recollect, but by the next few Sundays, Rev. Jamison had assumed all pastoral duties.

Remember the nine whose names appeared on the official injunction document? They all received letters from Rev. Jamison demanding that they appear before the pastor and deacons within twenty-four hours. Rev. Jamison had summoned them to his *court*!

Trustee Walton received a letter. Walton knew Rev. Jamison wrote the letter, but the tone of the letter coming from a religious leader, man of the cloth, as Rev. Jamison calls himself, Walton saw as a paradox.

Walton clearly understood. He knew what Rev. Jamison had said at the Joint Board meeting.

Trustee Walton said, "God understands too."

Rev. Jamison's letter received no response.

Each Sunday after that, Rev. Jamison preached about taking church business to court.

His followers appeared happy to hear that theme.

For the rest of the year and part of the next, that's what Rev. Jamison preached.

Reality...only Roberta and Thomas stayed around to hear him. The other seven plaintiffs wanted no part of C.O.H. They left.

Not only did those seven leave, but also fifty others left and found new church homes and another thirty members just stopped coming.

The retaliatory sermons kept on coming, but so did Roberta and Thomas.

Additionally, Roberta and Thomas had mastered a difficult skill. They knew how to accept the positive from church worship and pray for those who showed hostility.

And, the atmosphere provided plenty opportunity for them to pray.

Within a month, Rev. Jamison made an important announcement. He told the congregation about his upcoming wedding.

"I will be married before my installation."

His followers applauded his announcement with real enthusiasm and great joy.

"I expect each of you to do your part."

The congregation listened intently.

"I will have a wife, a son in college and a daughter in middle school. That requires more money. I will tax each adult member one hundred dollars and children just fifteen."

No one said *Amen!*

A few throats began to clear *uh, uh, uh.* What happened to the enthusiasm and joy?

A second letter…January 21st. Rev. Jamison made an attempt to communicate more effectively with the nine. Even some of Rev. Jamison's main supporters complained about the tone of the first letter.

However, no official questioned Rev. Jamison's tactics publicly.

Trustee Stove and Roberta decided to meet with Rev. Jamison and the deacons.

Jones and Stove wanted to hear just what Rev. Jamison would say. They also wanted to express their candid views.

On the evening of the meeting, Jones and Stove found Jamison and the deacons waiting in the pastor's office. Rev. Jamison and his deacons rose as Jones and Stove entered and remained standing for prayer. If Jones and Stove had not understood politics, they might have been impressed with the standing praying ceremony, they both said later.

Soon Rev. Jamison nodded for Mrs. Jones to begin talking. And, talk she did!

"Rev. Jamison, I am here at your second request."

Roberta, experienced with heated conferencing, knew exactly what she needed to say. Her daily routine often includes this kind of conference.

Trustee Stove, an experienced businessman and retired steelworker, knew how to express his feelings too.

Both indicated they had nothing against Rev. Jamison, personally, but they had a different preference for a pastor. Unlike the deacon board leadership, both Jones and Stove had lived through years of Rev. Jamison's pastorage at C.O.H.

They voiced their convictions openly, stating that they had not committed any crimes or sins.

No deacon spoke a word. I guess they came to protect the pastor from those *publicans and heathens* as stated in the second letter. Whatever their reason, they kept silent.

Reverend said, "You just can't walk back up in here like nothing has ever happened. You must apologize to me, the officials, and the church."

"Rev. Jamison, why do you follow certain rules and guidelines and pick out certain scriptures in the Bible to support what you think it says as you need it?" remarked Roberta.

Rev. Jamison answered, "You pounce on things when they jump out at you."

"That's probably true," Roberta said, "and from where I sit you constantly contradict yourself, making your leadership less effective."

She went on to say, "an apology is a sincere statement of regret for wrong doings. It's no joke! I would agree to an apology if I felt that I did something wrong. I chose to allow my name to be placed on the injunction document. That was my United States constitutional right. Having an opportunity to vote for the pastor, was my church constitutional right. I could not allow voting to be belittled. Besides that, the National Christian Living Baptist Convention, the highest organization of the Baptists, guarantees me that privilege. I did not wrong anybody. That act did not constitute a sin. I merely used my rights in a peaceful way to correct a wrong. The Bible speaks of resolving differences peacefully.

"I needed the court to protect my voting responsibility. As you know the PC had changed the rules to fit their personal choice, you. Through the court, I reclaimed my right to vote and the rights of other members as well. Did you know Deacon Smith and the members of the PC refused to listen to us?

"After the passage of the Voting Rights Act in 1968, I thought all God's children held voting dear to their hearts.

"Smith and Harris would be the first to say 'the man didn't allow us to vote.' Still they failed to see beyond the literal meaning of the law. It is difficult for me to understand Blacks denying other Blacks a chance to vote, especially in our church. I could not sit back and tolerate abuse like this as a citizen, a Christian woman, a charter member, and a counselor.

"I am not sure if the two of us are the only ones in this meeting tonight who chose to use the courts because of a serious church conflict.

"Despite what took place at the supervised church meeting, you say you are pastor. I accept that. Finally, anyone having a problem with anything I did, or anything I said tonight, I'll pray for them."

Silence swept the pastor's office. Rev. Jamison had anticipated coordinating a public apology. He had no intention of dealing with anything else. He nodded for Stove to begin.

"Roberta so beautifully expressed herself. I, too, know I have done no wrongs. Reverend, you told us you put all this behind, and you asked the church officials to do the same. What happened? Are you a man of your word? Can we the members trust what you say?"

Silence crept in again.

Rev. Jamison didn't answer the questions, but he did say something. He knew what he had just heard. Rev. Jamison realized what awaited him had he tried to answer.

"Let's pray," was all Rev. Jamison could utter, except for the prayer itself. And, "This meeting is now adjourned."

The Sunday following, Rev. Jamison exclaimed in his sermon: "God has three reasons for getting rid of certain church members. First, He gets rid of those who are independent.... They don't need God. Second, He eliminates the scared.... He can't use them. And third, He puts out the unrestrained.... Those individuals do things for selfish reasons."

Who had been selfish in this situation?

I sat thinking, Christians believe everybody needs God! Christians further believe God can change fear to confidence and hand anyone a giving heart. Oh well, God may get blamed for others indiscretions; Christians, don't worry; He can handle it!

The installation went as planned the following Wednesday, Thursday, Friday, and Saturday evenings.

Sunday morning and Sunday evening were included too. Yes...six different services with six different sermons and one extra preacher for each gathering to give words of encouragement. Hopefully, at least one speaker used contents from the book of Jude!

The church accepted the new Mrs. Leroy Jamison. She brought with her a pleasant personality and a strong second soprano voice.

I attended the 11:00 o'clock Sunday morning service.

Crowd...was it scarce that morning!

About a month later...Rev. Jamison yelled into the microphone, "If you can't give as God has instructed you, keep your little old money to yourself. We don't need it. We can make it without your little bit."

I continued to write my check. But one member sitting near me tore her $50 check up and placed the tiny pieces into her purse. That person rewrote a $50 check to a senior citizen sitting nearby who needed financial assistance.

By this time the musician had begun to play *You Can't Beat God's Giving*. The pastor and deacons began to parade around from the altar to the back, walking and singing, those who could, *no matter how you try*. They then came up the center aisle, followed by the entire congregation, which started from the back, walking up the two outer aisles, simultaneously, meeting center front, at the tray, returning via the center aisle, one line going right and the other left, as they returned to their seats. The singers completed the processional hastily coming from the choir loft to those same outer aisles, meeting in the center, two deep, making their way to the collection trays and back to the choir loft, thus completing the money and fashion parade.

Charles received the highest recognition. Rev. Jamison announced he had appointed him to the deacon ministry along with his Uncle Joe, first cousin Roscoe, and Frank Phillips, a member C.O.H. had accepted through the prison ministry.

Guess who joined church today? Reeia Buckman! Rev. Jamison appeared filled with the Holy Ghost as he took in his ex-sister-in-law. Quickly the congregation picked up the pastor's tone and rejoiced with him. No one could tell from the outward appearance who proved happier, Rev. Jamison or his staunch followers, that his ex-sister-in-law joined and became one of his members.

Chapter 21

October 21, 1986

One, two, three…maybe six members sang in the Senior Choir on October 21st.

What disappointment! C.O.H. once had voices that equaled the best in Chicago, New York or even Los Angeles.

Understandably, those choir members who breathed unhappy tones with the church, sat out or just failed to show up.

I couldn't believe the empty pews! Where did the happy souls go? Of course, the inactive individuals the defendants recruited to vote did not show up.

Needless to say, tithes and offerings trimmed tremendously. But as the Baptists say, *don't judge a church by the size of the congregation or the plate; it's the spiritual portion that counts.*

Those few members who attended rejoiced with tears. Rev. Jamison, too, exuberantly displayed his emotions. Nothing else could have been more important than securing a job.

Rev. Jamison had a love for the latest fashions; he could be called, at times, a non-traditional dresser! One Sunday he showed up in the pulpit in a tailored, bright, royal blue suit. The accessories included a white shirt with a bright red and blue tie-handkerchief set. He had the handkerchief triangular shaped in the upper right jacket pocket. His shoes and socks matched too, navy socks and patent leather shoes. The shoes showed a reflection of his picture. How is that for clergy class?

Regardless of what he wore, at the end of sermons, Deacon Barnes always jumped to the pulpit to help Rev. Jamison put on his robe, a batman cape, as the 1980's teens called it.

Lead me Lord, lead me in Thy righteousness,
Make Thy way plain before Thy face.

In spite of a touching introduction Rev. Jamison inadvertently executed before each message, he preached sermons like these:

November 3$^{rd:}$ *The Payback: Disconnect with the Enemy*
November 17th: *How to Treat Your Enemies and Praise God's Man*
December 18th: *How to Wean the Bad and Sinful in Our Church*

Each Sunday these words guided those accused.

"HOW BEAUTIFUL ARE THE FEET OF THEM THAT PREACH THE GOSPEL OF PEACE." (Romans 10:15)

By January, Rev. Jamison called for the semi-annual church meeting. He had indicated that he had some serious matters to execute. I told my sister Lorene what to expect in the meeting.

Ronald, who came to church whenever his medical school schedule allowed him, discussed the same with his aunt as he left church that third Sunday in December. "Well, Aunt Lorene, Rev. Jamison has made plans to turn my dad, Aunt Roberta and the other seven out of church."

"Ronnie, you missed the point of his sacred message. He preached the Bible today."

"Oh, yes!" Ronald replied.

"He would never do anything like that," she said.

To that Ronald replied, "Aunt Lorene, I don't have problems with comprehending anything that the Rev. preaches. He plans to K-I-C-K them O-U-T, the bad and sinful."

January brought bitter, cold temperatures that year. January 14th had a minus zero temperature. Twenty-seven members managed to clear the snow and ice from their frozen cars and fight nature's frigid weather as they made it to C.O.H. The cold weather proved just what God sent Rev. Jamison's supporters who wanted no direct part of the plan. When Rev. Jamison presented his proposal to only twenty-seven members, he looked for at least one verbal member to help him accomplish his mission.

Sister Sanders bounced out from her seat to her feet. "Pastor Jamison," she hailed. "Yes, Sister Sanders," Rev. Jamison cried. "I move that the church dismiss all members whose names appeared on the court injunction from…church."

Mrs. Wilson jumped to her feet. "Honorable Pastor Jamison!"

"Yes, Madam Wilson," he said.

"I second that motion!" The motion carried twenty-three to four.

Lorene told the church how illegal the action appeared to be. "Only one person signed the court document. Your actions appear unfounded on solid legal ground." I suppose she suggested that further action could be challenged in a court of law. She knew the real person Rev. Jamison sought had left by then and united with another Baptist church.

Mrs. Wilson rose again. "No excuses! No excuses! They may not have signed the court papers, but they gave permission for their names to be placed on it." Mrs. Wilson walked away speaking something to herself. She uttered in a soft tone, "Put them out. We don't need them. We don't need their help doing nothing here anymore."

To that Rev. Jamison replied in a smooth, calm voice, "You must separate the good from the bad. That's what God wants of you. Christians must not associate with the evil ones."

After the church meeting, no one in attendance knew anything about the action taken except those four who voted against Rev. Jamison's dismissal proposal. The defendants and their supporters tried to protect Rev. Jamison. Besides, they didn't want the plaintiffs and their supporters to know that they had been misled again.

Somehow the entire Grand Rapids ministry community knew about Rev. Jamison's action. Several community friends confronted me about our church news.

Within a few days after the church meeting, Rev. Jamison wrote to the nine:

"As pastor of Church of Heaven Christian Living Baptist, I regret to inform you that you were voted out of membership at our semi-annual church meeting by a majority of the membership on January 14, 1987."

Could twenty-three be called a majority?

Sister Sanders informed church members after the letter, her motion did not include dismissal. According to her story, she declared a motion to dismiss the plaintiffs from church organizations and leadership roles. However, the membership remained silent and accepted Rev. Jamison's actions.

Trustee Walton, upon receipt of his first letter, called his three adult sons, Thomas, Jr., Elwood and Ronald. Each expressed to his father how proud he felt to be the son of a man who stood up for sound, moral principles in the church. The trustee admired their comments.

"What an example you are for us," they all implied.

Chapter 22

June 06, 1987

Additional members began dropping out after the dismissal. They joined other churches…Baptist, Jehovah's Witness, Methodist, Church of God…you name it. Those movements placed C.O.H. under high x-ray radiation in the community. What a difficult time for C.O.H.! For those who left, they decided to avoid the bittersweet. I regretted seeing other church members scatter, but religious worship is a personal matter.

"WOE *BE UNTO THE PASTORS THAT DESTROY AND SCATTER THE SHEEP OF MY PASTURE! SAITH THE LORD*. (Jeremiah 23:1)

Bobbie has often said, "I'll return to the church I love as soon as Rev. Jamison leaves. Until then, I'll pray for my sins, and request others to pray for me as I visit other churches."

Trustee Walton showed real stamina. He did not yield, nor did he cease to pray. He often quoted, **"WAIT ON THE LORD: BE OF GOOD COURAGE…."** (Psalm 27:14) His position forced others, even me, to take a deeper look at his actions. However, I always knew deeds, not flowery words, define Christian character.

"I understand the story of Job," the trustee commented.

"…I SHALL NOT BE MOVED." (Psalm 10:6)

I told my husband, "I will leave with you and join another church."

To that he continued, **"AND HE SHALL BE LIKE A TREE PLANTED BY THE RIVERS OF WATER."** (Psalm 1:3)

"…BE YE STEADFAST, UNMOVABLE, ALWAYS ABOUNDING IN THE WORK OF THE LORD…." (I Corinthians 15:58)

By June 6th I wrote Rev. Jamison a letter: (I went to my Christian brother.) I communicated that I cared about the church (people) and the church's direction.

Further, I explained that I understood human interactions and reactions. So, I volunteered to assist in finding a solution to the situation.

The next Sunday I asked Rev. Jamison about a response during the visitors' welcome. He did his usual smile and started a conversation.

C.O.H. had just lost two active members, Deacon Billy Packson and his wife Pattie, to another Grand Rapids Baptist church. The top church leader embarrassed the deacon's wife. Mrs. Packson, a church nurse, brought orange juice to an elderly diabetic member in need of services during preaching time. The leader did not understand. He questioned her actions from the pulpit. After that the Nurses' Guild assigned another person to that task.

Selina returned to the choir. She has two elementary school age children to train. I applauded her!

Realizing the condition of the church, the directress of Christian training arranged family conferences with the pastor. This arrangement included the extended family...mother, father, adult children, and their spouses... everybody. Few participated because the members felt the leaders at C.O.H. had decided to do their own thing. Relationships continued to be edgy.

Pearl had been considered a well-read Bible scholar. She instructed the Sunday school teachers, a position she loved. One could depend on her. She knew the Bible, although some members felt she handled herself as though she alone had all the correct answers. According to many members, if anyone's answers conflicted with hers, she would say, "You are wrong, brother!"

Pearl continued this approach until one of her answers did not match that of Rev. Jamison's. The lesson...adultery! Pearl got fired from her post.

The pastor and Trustee Carr had a full-blown blowout! In the past, trustees have assisted the pastor in shoveling snow at the parsonage. When Trustee Carr's turn rolled around, to lend a hand, Carr replied, "Rev. is a man just like me and about my age. He can shovel his own damn snow."

Deacon Barnes told Rev. Jamison about Carr's statement.

Rev. Jamison said to Carr, "Did you say I could shovel my own d— snow?"

Carr said, "Yes, I said it."

"I need an apology from you," said Rev. Jamison. Carr had got caught up in the forced apologizing game.

"I am sorry, because I said it in front of several ladies," Carr told Rev. Jamison. But Carr knew Rev. Jamison would kick him out of church too.

The friction has been brewing off and on since then.

Rev. Jamison announced, "Today is our organist's last day." The church gave a farewell to him.

September 27th Rev. Jamison made an appeal to the membership. "We need money! I must ask you to give a sacrificial offering today in addition to what you had planned to give." No one explained the purpose or why this great need occurred. "I will begin with $50," Rev. Jamison stated. About sixty persons responded without any further explanation. The unknown urgency didn't bother them at all. "Come put the sacrificial offering in first and return to your seat. Then come a second time to bring your gift for today," he went on to say. Two trustees had been asked to stand, hold trays on each side of the church for the sacrificial offering.

Rev. Jamison chose not to preach that day. One of his associates delivered the message. If another preacher brings the message, the members must pay. After the sermon, Rev. Jamison said, "We must give a love offering to the man of God; I'll start with $10. I'm asking all of you to stand and march around to contribute to this love offering."

This time the audience, for the most part, remained seated. In a raised voice the pastor said, " I know you are going to obey me and pay for the word of God."

The morning announcements indicated that Rev. Jamison had accepted an invitation to preach at a church at 4:00 p.m. and another at 7:00 p.m. I read about his anticipated appearances at those local churches in the morning newspaper.

He had plenty of pep the next Sunday! Rev. Jamison preached a stirring sermon, ***True Love for Jesus***.

"Preach Jamison, preach." Deacon Johnson said waving his cane.

The pastor spoke of love for self, love for others, love for our neighbors and love for God's work. He even mentioned how important it is to treat everybody with respect and dignity.

As he came to a close and the choir began to sing acappella, I thought I heard someone walking down the center aisle when Rev. Jamison announced the invitation to Christian discipleship.

Come to Jesus, Come to Jesus....
Just now, just now....

By that time I discerned a person coming down the aisle from the middle rear of the sanctuary. I could not recognize the individual from the far-left side where I sat. I figured I did not know that person.

The choir continued but in a sacred, melodious tone, with the congregation joining.

He will save you...He will save you, just now...

The female, well dressed, arrived at the front altar. She wore a white wide-rimmed hat, and a white tee length dress. The striking gold jewelry she wore gave her a rich look. Besides, she walked with grace and confidence in her Fifth Avenue looking off-white pumps. She then extended her right hand to the pastor. When this lady, ready to confess, did an about face or turn around, I then recognized this one who had come! Mrs. Bobbye Grass Jamison!

"WATCH AND PRAY, THAT YE ENTER NOT INTO TEMPTATION: THE SPIRIT INDEED IS WILLING, BUT THE FLESH IS WEAK. " (Matthew 26:41)

Chapter 23

April 23, 1990

Children, dressed in shades of blue, pink and yellow trimmed with varying materials and designs of white, lit up the sanctuary like a church Easter parade!

Trustee Walton and I usually took a spring vacation during this time. But this time, we chose to stay home.

I thought about visiting another church. So, I mentioned the visiting idea to Trustee Walton. He immediately said, "No, let's go to C.O.H!"

I replied O.K., but my mind still hassled with memories of 1985 Easter Sunday at C.O.H. Therefore, at that moment, I gave an O.K. answer just for formality to satisfy my husband. Actually, I had no intentions of going to C.O.H. on Easter Sunday.

C.O.H.'s annual children's Easter program had been cancelled. The congregation braced itself to miss the insurmountable joys the children bring from their Easter program. The group had settled to bypass the innocent spirit the children represent when performing. But we longed to see them perform.

Easter Sunday morning Rev. Jamison pleased the congregation with, "The children have been included in today's order of worship."

I loved that! The fathers, mothers, grandparents, friends and congregation did too!

Selina and Mrs. Jamison, the first lady, directed the children, ages four through high school, in a presentation of *"He Is Risen as He Said!"*

The pre-schoolers stole the spotlight holding sacred symbols: a cross, sword, cloth, and cup.

The upper elementary and teenagers read the scripts.

Wow! How uplifting! How refreshing!

Rev. Jamison concluded the service with a mini sermon. He reinforced the crucifixion and resurrection themes. The picture he painted gave who, when, where and how of the crucifixion and resurrection.

I felt proud that I attended C.O.H!

Immediately after the benediction, as Trustee Walton, Roberta, Tracy and I got up from our seats to leave, Deacon Smith and Deacon Harris approached us. We had always sat together for support during the three-year ordeal!

Deacon Harris began to speak, "We have decided to restore both of you to the church."

Neither Trustee Walton nor Roberta spoke a word. Both stood attentively speechless!

Deacon Smith said, "Yes, we have been working on this for a while."

Trustee Walton and Roberta continued to listen intently. Tracy and I did too.

I waited to hear the word apology. I did, in fact, hear it.

"No apology is required," Deacon Harris uttered.

This had been a stressful time for our family. So, a sigh of relief swept over me as if a powerful whirlwind blew over.

One little tear somehow forced its way to my eyes, followed by thousands, which completely blinded my view.

I could not tell how Trustee Walton, Roberta or Tracy reacted, but they had to feel the presence of our supreme being!

"An announcement will be made Sunday to the membership." Harris indicated.

I was happy to hear that! I wanted to yell, "Thank you Jesus!"

Deacon Harris also stated, "Both of you must be restored to all ministries or committees you served on before your inappropriate dismissal."

Trustee Walton said, "Now I can give service to C.O.H, the church of my choice."

Roberta stated, "I am willing and ready to continue my volunteer work as I promised that I would serve Him until I die."

"The record will show no interruption in your membership," cried Deacon Smith.

Tracy said, "May God bless us all," as we left the edifice.

"AND WHEN THEY LOOKED, THEY SAW THAT THE STONE WAS ROLLED AWAY: FOR IT WAS GREAT." (Mark 16:4)

J. Moffett Walker

EPILOGUE

The new C.O.H. proved to be a congregation with few faithful members struggling for mere survival. Regretfully, spiritual and emotional abuse did occur. On the other hand, a majority of the present parishioners denied this allegation. Although the members saw what happened, some chose to remain loyal to the leaders. Moreover, to see and remain silent shows denial. To deny and suppress set the tone for continued abuse without a need for a change. So, Church of Heaven's leadership and congregation represent an unhealthy wave that has somehow found its way into too many congregations.

Actually, this church symbolizes the kinds of struggles and abuses that exist in churches across the country, especially the Christian Living Baptist churches. Unfortunately, many struggles have been caused by unethical acts knowingly or unknowingly committed by the leaders. Besides, some congregations have no recourse for filing grievances for leaders' wrong doings! The setup suggests only members will do wrong.

Meanwhile, the profile of C.O.H., according to the story, questioned the status of the organization. The leaders' action and followers' reaction placed C.O.H. farther away from a true Christian Living Baptist Church. Sadly, the leaders didn't seem to see that picture.

Take a comprehensive look at these occurrences: 1) The leadership began to have secret meetings with only selected deacons and invited trustees. 2) The leaders had near zero tolerance for professional or college trained visiting ministers. Not only that, but the same non-acceptance applied to the majority of the middle class members. 3) The PC played games with certain prospective pastoral candidates, encouraging them to withdraw their applications. 4) The Pulpit Committee members took it upon themselves to reject the pastor-elect and hire their choice for pastor. 5) Yet, enough active members kept their devotion to the abusive leadership. 6) Leaders kept changing the order of worship to advance their agenda. 7) The chairman of the PC misinformed the congregation about his church business interaction with the pastor-elect. Smith wrote Rev. Clark a letter stating that the church had changed its position about the pastor-elect, while telling the congregation that Clark would begin his duties in early March. 8) The leaders abandoned the church's constitution. However, they used portions of the constitution when an issue promoted their agendas as they perceived it. 9) Unwritten rules became the mode of operation. No one knew what to expect next. Guidelines...none except what the leaders said. 10) The members of the PC remained loyal to Deacon Smith. 11) After hiring Rev. Jamison, officials paid him with church funds despite a civil court's ruling and later continued paying him after being warned by the judge. 12) The officials, including Rev. Jamison, failed to be truthful about their involvement in the overthrow. Regretfully, their testimonies went unchallenged in the civil court system. 13) After the court supervised church meeting, Rev. Jamison called a meeting of the Joint Board. He initiated a compromise with the leaders to "let by-gones be by-gones" for the good of all. He indicated no one would be dismissed because of the injunction. He changed his position. 14) Somehow, Rev. Jamison used only twenty-four votes in a semi-annual church meeting to dismiss the nine plaintiffs. [Such a legal vote would have required two-thirds of the membership, according to the constitution] 15) Three years later the officials apologized to Trustee Walton and Roberta, the two remaining plaintiffs. The other seven plaintiffs had united with other churches although one was deceased by then.

What Is A Church?

A church is a safe place where people assemble to worship. The building may be called temple, synagogue, kingdom hall, cathedral or a tent. It matters not! What matters are the relationships the people inside the physical structure have one to another. Since the building is merely a structure, it has no purpose, except housing the people. Therefore, all congregations need a check and balance system for members and officials, including the pastor. C.O.H.'s congregation had failed to do this.

A church is God's house! On a greater level, the Christians in a church are involved in programs to help society. For example, church programs help direct and train the young, revitalize the God like spirit of the old, and reach out to the needy, sick and shut-in. But if leaders say one thing and live another, that will only send mixed messages and confuse members, especially the young, thereby causing a decline in morality.

Additionally, the leaders of church programs must set examples for others with their lives, morally, socially, and spiritually. Effective officials lead by example. Church leaders, who fail to lead by the examples they verbalize, weaken their effectiveness. But those leaders who live by principles of love can and should expect others to follow them. Effective church leaders know that failure to practice what they teach take away the right to expect positive results from others. Those leaders who live by the religious principles help create harmony, togetherness and oneness within the congregation.

This philosophy by no means suggests a pastor or any other religious leader must have a perfect record. But it does mean a religious leader who commits the same immoral acts over and over again needs to either change his or her action or quit the ministry or any other official leadership roles.

Is There A Clear Message for Congregations?

There will always be a need for the church! Obviously the need for cults exists not! But do you agree that they exist? Our society needs our church leaders and members to verbalize and practice the golden rule: "Do unto others as you would have them do unto you." The younger generation watches adults every move, good or bad, right or wrong. Therefore, effective church leaders are needed to help develop and maintain society's desired values. In the meantime, the method of selecting church deacons needs reevaluating. Usually, the pastors select the deacons in the Christian Living Churches. Consequently, churches have fewer principle-oriented leaders. As a result, the deacons sit back and allow the pastors to do their own thing. Hopefully, this selection method will change soon to a more practical method.

What Is the Real Purpose of Church Splits?

One easy way to feel successful after an overthrow is to establish a new church. The plaintiffs and their supporters decided against that. Admittedly, that has been a tradition! Moreover, C.O.H. became a church through a church split.

Most plaintiffs and their supporters had experienced the joys and aches of establishing a new church. Besides, the plaintiffs and their supporters knew what that meant! With a Christian Living Baptist Church on practically every street corner in the city, another one would mean further division within the community. Practically every small church in Grand Rapids represents a split from another. Could church splits be categorized as cynical games? What do splits say for religion? What do they say for Black religious leadership? What do they say for congregations? Do splits suggest the lack of appropriate structure? Do church splits mean unresolved power struggles? Well, stability in the Black community is a century-old overdue library book!

What the Christian Living Baptist Church needs is not another split, but sound leadership from the national organization and within each congregation. With these two, Christian Living Baptist churches will likely experience **unconditional** stability.

Today's churches in conflict, show reasonable guidelines once set forth and followed have taken back seats to intrepid or bold pulpit punks running the whole show. The cunning preachers control, misuse, abuse, misappropriate funds and knowingly misinterpret scriptures for his or her own personal gains…master manipulators. Additionally, females, who make up a majority of the Christian Living Baptist congregations, need to face the challenges discussed in **Church Folk** now! Being in majority places this responsibility on the females. So, in essence, females cannot be selfish; nor can females afford to sit back and just watch. Females can no longer become involved in or accept immoral acts. As chosen ones, females must work within the present structure to correct the wrongs and change them to rights for the children and the community. Being a majority carries with it this moral obligation.

What Did the Injunction Accomplish?

Members who filed the injunction against the leadership lost the case...or did they? The group filed the injunction because the membership had no voice in the selection of a pastor. Well, the injunction restored all members' voting privileges. How significant for everyone! Too bad that the defendant supporters failed to see beyond the person they wanted for pastor that time. Their then present wants blinded their tomorrow's needs. One pastor in Grand Rapids dismissed three members ages 78, 87 and 90 from a Methodist congregation. He had encountered a conflict with them. But the check and balance system restored their memberships. Yet, in another denomination the pastor learned that he could not dismiss those he saw as causing trouble. Sixteen members had asked their pastor to give the church a schedule of his weekly activities. So, he directed the minister of music to dismiss them from the choir where they volunteered their time and services. In a third congregation, $500,000 disappeared like magic when the new pastor arrived. In a fourth Baptist congregation, a pastor took sexual advantage of a minor female member, and the congregation blamed the child!

Further, the injunction pioneered through the wilderness, a deep-rooted silver trail of non-tolerance for wrong doings in the Christian Living Baptist Church. How profoundly symbolic! One reason for the symbolism is, Christian Living Baptists have been taught from and old unwritten rule that God would somehow punish members who question and expose confusion in their churches!

That seed which the plaintiffs planted, no doubt, will come up in the souls of the new C.O.H. members and other congregations too when the iron curtains of injustice fall on them and **reality** says hello!

"I HAVE PLANTED, APOLLOS WATERED; BUT GOD GAVE THE INCREASE. SO THEN NEITHER IS HE THAT PLANTETH ANYTHING, NEITHER HE THAT WATERETH; GOD THAT GIVETH THE INCREASE." (1 Corinthians 3:6-7)

About the Author

Juanita Moffett Walker, teacher and counselor, states, "Society can no longer expect schools solely to shoulder the load of educating children in the 21st century." Besides parents, she believes churches have a unique responsibility too. The author further inferred, a precious few congregations have begun to tap their resources. However, she feels the young church members need their congregations to help them with leadership training, internet safety, citizenship reinforcement, effective mentoring, academic tutoring, and job shadowing. But, the writer says, "The possibility of churches interweaving an education ministry into their youth programs, using their own resources, has gone basically untapped!"

"My parents, who lived in Mississippi where I grew up, required me to attend church regularly and to participate in activities. The training I received there has been indispensable. Consequently, my husband, Tommy, and I welcomed the guidance our Indiana church gave our now three adult sons." Nevertheless, when this writer began keeping a log of happenings in her community, a disturbing profile emerged. Therefore, she captured her findings to share in a tell-all novel, *Church Folk*. "I wrote this first person point of view novel to enlighten, inspire and cultivate critical thinking about the needs within congregations, but especially the multi-dimensional Afro-American religious world," the author concluded.

The author resides in Gary, Indiana.